Economics Through Everyday Life

To Elaine Bensavage,
Boban Rakovic, &
Ed Easterling

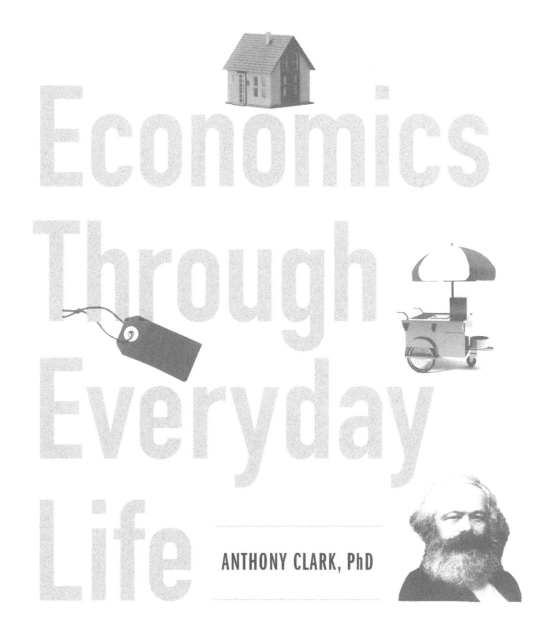

Economics Through Everyday Life

ANTHONY CLARK, PhD

FROM CHINA & CHILI DOGS TO MARX & MARIJUANA

ZEPHYROS PRESS

CONTENTS

ECONOMICS

GLOBALIZATION

BUSINESS

MARKETS

BOOMS & BUBBLES

REGULATIONS

MACROECONOMICS

MONOPOLIES

HEALTHCARE

CAPITAL

INTRODUCTION

The financial crisis of 2007–2008 took a lot of Americans by surprise. Many people saw their retirement savings drop rapidly in value. Business owners found it difficult to get loans from banks. A recession followed the crisis, and many workers in a wide range of industries lost their jobs.

The financial crisis and the ensuing events were a wake-up call for economists, who began to ask themselves what they had missed, and for policymakers in Washington who realized that some kind of immediate action was necessary to prevent the economy from spiraling further downward. It was also a wake-up call for many ordinary Americans who, perhaps for the first time in their lives, got a small taste of the kind of economic pain that their parents, grandparents, or great-grandparents had experienced during the Great Depression. It was as if the United States had been on autopilot, the entire nation taking for granted that the economy would keep growing, that money would keep flowing from the banks, and that companies would keep expanding and hiring workers.

And the financial crisis brought something else—new (or renewed) and widespread interest in economics. Many people suddenly had lots of economic questions: *Can things get worse? Can the United States experience another Great Depression? Who is to blame? Wall Street bankers? The Federal Reserve? The government?* There were more specific questions, too: *What does the Federal Reserve do, anyway? Is there really a problem with income inequality in America? How can we keep the Social Security program solvent and intact for future generations?*

These questions, among many others, are addressed in this book. Economics isn't just for academics, government policymakers, or Wall Street titans. The field actually has a lot to offer non experts, too. When you understand economics, even at a very basic level, you can make better economic decisions for yourself, and you can be a more informed citizen when it comes to deciding how and when the federal government should be involved in the economy.

With these thoughts in mind, this book has two main purposes. The first is to tell you about the most important economic terms and principles in the clearest way possible, and with little economic jargon, so you can develop a grasp of the important economic concepts that every informed citizen should understand. The second is to present you with as nonpartisan and balanced an analysis as possible of some of the most important economic issues affecting our country today, so you'll have the information you need to reach your own conclusions.

CHAPTER 1 introduces some basic terms and concepts in the field of economics, and includes a brief overview of the major schools of economic thought.

CHAPTER 2 builds on that foundation by laying out additional basic concepts and helping you learn to see the world the way economists do.

CHAPTER 3 offers an overview of what markets are and how they're supposed to operate. The chapter also discusses why government intervention in markets is sometimes needed.

CHAPTER 4 explores key concepts and issues related to competition, monopolies, and antitrust laws.

CHAPTER 5 examines economics in the context of globalization and international trade, while also touching on the economics of immigration.

CHAPTER 6 presents some of the basic measures that economists and policymakers use to stay informed about the state of the economy. The chapter also covers the basics of fiscal policy, monetary policy, and the workings of the Federal Reserve.

CHAPTER 7 discusses economic booms, bubbles, and busts, placing them in the broader context of business cycles. The chapter also examines the financial crisis of 2007–2008.

CHAPTER 8 takes a close look at the federal Social Security program, federal welfare programs, and the US healthcare system and how they affect the nation's taxpayers.

CHAPTER 9 offers some parting thoughts, as well as some predictions about what the field of economics will look like in the future, and the implications of economic research and thought.

After you've read the book, don't be surprised if you find yourself paying closer attention to economic news. You may even decide that you'd like to learn still more about economics. It's true that graphs, charts, and equations can look rather complex, but always keep a simple fact in mind: Most economic theories and concepts are simpler than economists make them appear. It doesn't take much to learn the essentials of economics—and the essentials will carry you a long way.

1 WHAT IS ECONOMICS & WHY DOES IT MATTER?

Since the 19th century, economics has borne the ignominious moniker of "the dismal science." Some people think economics is called "the dismal science" because it's a dry and difficult subject. Others think it's because economics tackles depressing topics such as poverty, crime, war, taxes, inflation, and economic collapse. The cheerless nickname has been attributed by some to the Scottish historian Thomas Carlyle, who reportedly coined the term when discussing economist Thomas Malthus's prediction that one day population growth would outstrip food production and cause widespread famine. It's true that Carlyle wrote about Malthus on occasion. But Carlyle's negative characterization of economics in fact appears in an article that he wrote about slavery in the West Indies, not in any of his writings about

"The Dismal Science"

Thomas Carlyle, who once called economics a "dismal science," also wrote books about the French Revolution and Frederick the Great.

Malthus. And, as it turns out, Carlyle delivered his insult to economics simply because the free market economists of his time did not support his proslavery views (see chapter 3 for a discussion of free markets). So, in the end, economics earned its less than auspicious nickname for being on what most would agree was the right side of history.

This first chapter will introduce you to a few very basic economic ideas, and will plant the seed in your mind that economics is anything but "dismal." You'll learn what economics is and what it isn't, and you'll learn about the fundamental problem at the heart of every economic question. In addition, you'll get a brief overview of the major schools of economic thought.

ECONOMICS DEFINED

What do economists do? A simple answer is that economists practice, teach, or work to advance the field of economics.

Every person who chooses finance or accounting as a college major is also required to study economics, but economics isn't the same as finance or accounting. Economics is the framework that underlies all the business disciplines, just as physics is the framework that underlies all the engineering disciplines.

A lot of economic work involves money, but it doesn't have to. That's why it would be a mistake to say that economics is the science of money. It's true that plenty of economists spend their careers studying money, the money supply, and the banking system, but a pile of money doesn't do anything by itself. What interests an economist is how human beings behave when they get their hands on a pile of money. In other words, economics is about human behavior.

Economics is not the only field concerned with the study of human behavior, of course. Psychology, sociology, and anthropology are three fields in the social sciences that also focus on human beings and how they behave. In this respect, then, economics is more closely aligned with those fields than with the fields of finance and accounting. We might say that economics is the social science concerned with how people (or other decision-making units such as business firms or government agencies) can best allocate their limited resources to achieve optimal or maximum satisfaction. Or, we could say that economics deals with how people make choices in conditions of **scarcity**.

ECONOMIC RESOURCES

Why is scarcity so important to economics? It's because economic resources are scarce—and that's the problem at the heart of every economic question.

Most modern economists start from the assumption that having more material goods is better than having fewer material goods. In making this assumption, economists are following not only the founders of economic

WHY MOST ECONOMISTS DON'T GIVE STOCK TIPS

Most investment firms have economists on staff, but an economist is not a stockbroker. In fact, many economists refuse to give advice on investments. First, although economists are generally paid well, only a few have struck it rich in the stock market. Second, the few economists who actually are wizards at reading and predicting the stock market are probably not eager to reveal their secrets. But the likely main reason they don't offer stock tips is because economists know that, on average, an expert picking stocks for a portfolio is no more likely to pick a winner than a monkey throwing darts at the stock pages.

Economic research supports a concept called the **efficient market hypothesis**, which states that it's impossible for anyone to pick a portfolio of stocks that beats the market. In other words, you cannot pick a portfolio that attains a return better than the average return in the market. Why is that? It's because all the relevant information about any stock has already been priced into that stock, and no one has access to any special information that would support a prediction of a particular stock's price going up or going down. To put this idea another way, no one can beat the market on a regular basis.

There are always exceptions to the rule, and one person who has managed to beat the market consistently is Warren Buffet, the so-called "Wizard of Omaha." However, in tests pitting professional brokers against stand-ins for monkeys—that is, either computers or ordinary people picking stock portfolios—the "monkeys" typically have done about as well as the pros, if not slightly better. (And stock-picking monkeys don't charge fees or work for commissions.)

Warren Buffet (left), meeting with President Obama (right) in 2010, became one of the world's richest men as the head of Berkshire Hathaway, a financial holdings firm.

THE HEDONIC TREADMILL:
WHY ENOUGH IS NEVER ENOUGH

Every government, business, household, and individual faces *some* degree of scarcity, no matter how much money is available. Not only that, but human beings who want a material good and then manage to acquire it will also have a tendency to want more and more of it. This tendency is known as **hedonic adaptation,** and it explains why some people never enjoy true happiness, no matter how rich or successful they become.

Let's take a common example: Joe wins $10 million in a state lottery, and for a little while he's a lot happier. But he quickly gets used to having that much money, and soon he wants even more. In fact, he actually comes to believe that $10 million is no longer enough to meet his needs. Joe has returned to his usual level of happiness— what might be called his *set point.*

We're all like Joe in our tendency to maintain a relatively stable level of happiness over time, even when some positive or negative event lifts us up or knocks us down. As a result, we're all putting in time on what economists, stealing a term from psychologists, call the *hedonic treadmill.* This is why scarcity will always be a reality for human beings, and why the field of economics matters.

thought but also many economists that have followed since, all of whom have observed that when people have a choice, they tend to prefer having more to having less.

Thus the more-is-better paradigm is fundamental to economics, although it is sometimes questioned and even criticized. For example, in 1973 E. F. Schumacher published his influential book *Small Is Beautiful* and gave it the subtitle *Economics as if People Mattered.* More recent movements—for tiny houses, or simple living—also seem to fly in the face of this basic economic assumption.

Remember, though, that economics is about studying human behavior. When economists observe that the typical human being has a more-is-better mind-set, they're not necessarily saying that it's best for people to adopt this attitude, or that it should permeate economics in the Western world. They're simply drawing a conclusion derived from hundreds of years of studying how actual human beings relate to actual material goods.

Economic resources are generally divided into four categories: land, labor, capital, and entrepreneurship. When economists talk about resources at the small-scale (micro) level, they're usually referring to the *assets,* or *inputs,* that allow a firm to produce goods and services to be sold in the market. When economists talk about economic resources at the

(Opposite) "Real capital," like farm equipment or computers used to support production, is differentiated from "financial capital," such as cash used to pay farm workers.

large-scale (macro) level, they're usually referring to the assets that allow a nation (or a state or region) to produce goods and services for citizens. Let's take a closer look at each of these four categories of economic resources.

- *Land* is more than the ground you walk on, and it's more than farmland. It includes any natural asset that may be used in producing goods and services. Water, trees, oil, and minerals all belong to the resource category of land.

- *Labor* is exactly what it sounds like— workers, along with their skills and

abilities. The resource category of labor also has a connection with the term *human capital*, which refers to workers' skills, experience, and education.

- The resource category of *capital* includes all goods produced in support of the production of other goods. Machinery (a tractor, for example), equipment (say, a computer), and business facilities (such as the office that houses the computer) are all included in the subcategory of *real capital*. Economists distinguish real capital from *financial capital*, which includes assets such as stocks, bonds, and cash.

- Over the years, *entrepreneurship* has come to be recognized as an additional resource category. The role of entrepreneurs in an economy is decidedly different from the role of workers. Entrepreneurs assemble material resources and determine production and distribution. They are innovators who dream up new products, create new twists to old products, and open new markets for established products. They also assume the risk of failure inherent in any business endeavor.

The stock of economic resources is always limited. Over time, however, new resources can be discovered or otherwise acquired. The quality of resources can also be improved. For example, when workers receive more training (i.e., when human capital increases), the workforce becomes more productive. When the stock of resources increases, or when the quality of resources improves, the result is economic growth.

Whatever the source of an economy's growth, most people would agree that a growing economy is better than a stagnating or declining economy. That's because trade-offs have to be made when an economy is stagnant or, even worse, shrinking, and often those trade-offs require tough political choices. Where should we cut spending—in the area of healthcare or in education? Do we close this naval base or that army base? But when the economy is growing, not only can we keep both bases open, we can also build a brand-new Air Force base while also improving the quality of healthcare and education.

A growing economy also lowers the unemployment rate by boosting the supply of jobs. And who doesn't want low unemployment? At the household level, long-term unemployment can be devastating for an individual or a family, and high unemployment in the larger society is associated with many problems, including social unrest. That's why the financial media follow the unemployment rate so closely, why politicians give it so much attention, and why economic policy—at the national level and often at the state and local levels as well—is generally geared to boosting the economy and reducing unemployment.

SCHOOLS AND SUBFIELDS OF ECONOMICS

At any given point in history, economists have rarely been in total agreement about what constitutes the best economic policy. Because economics is a social science, which means that its theories can't be tested in highly controlled laboratories, there has probably been more disagreement among economists than among colleagues in the hard sciences. As a result, there are numerous schools of economic thought and, economists being economists, they can't even agree on exactly how many schools of thought there are. Some schools have marked similarities while some are polar opposites, but each one constitutes a particular way of looking at the economy and economic policy.

A good place to start our discussion on schools of economic thought is the concept of mercantilism and the system derived from that concept. The mercantilist system dominated Europe from the 1500s to the 1700s, and it was marked by heavy government regulation of trade. That heavy regulation had a single purpose: to strengthen the hand of the state. Nations that took the mercantilist approach sought to export goods and block imports. These governments also tended to hoard gold and silver. One hallmark of the mercantilist system was colonialism, particularly when it came to plundering the resources of colonized regions. No modern-day economist would be likely to identify as a mercantilist, but mercantilist ideas do crop up among politicians who promote restrictions on imports.

Major Schools of Economic Thought

This summary doesn't presume to cover every possible school of economic thought—there may be dozens, thanks to economists' tendency to split hairs. Instead, this summary is intended to give you an idea of the breadth of economics and the nature of its internal conversations, or discourse. Even Nobel laureates in economics sharply disagree with one another. That's one reason why you, as an informed citizen, should have a basic understanding of what's at stake in those disagreements, so that you can listen to both sides and arrive at your own conclusions.

YOU CAN'T MAKE AN OMELETTE WITHOUT SOMEONE TO SHIP EGGS

When Adam Smith published the famous book known today as *The Wealth of Nations*, he observed that people pursuing their own economic interests inevitably promote society's interests. He noted that, when left alone, people would seek to maximize profit and revenue by developing efficient production and charging low prices, thereby benefitting both the seller and the buyer. Since then, people have often cast Smith as an 18th-century prototype of Gordon Gekko, the fictional stockbroker in the film *Wall Street* who said, in effect, that greed is good. But that's not quite what Smith meant.

Consider everything that has to happen for a carton of eggs to appear in your local supermarket. Someone has to produce lumber and wire and ship those materials to a place where someone else can buy them to build chicken coops. Someone has to produce chicken feed. A farmer has to raise the chickens and harvest their eggs. Meanwhile, others have to build oil rigs so gasoline can fuel the trucks that will have to be manufactured before the eggs can be transported to the supermarket in the carton that someone has to fabricate.

Isn't every one of these people pursuing a personal economic interest? And isn't every one of them also promoting society's interests?

But who is coordinating all this activity?

No one. It's all occurring as if it were being guided by an unseen power. This power is what Adam Smith called the market's "invisible hand," and what modern economists recognize as market forces.

The Classical School

It's generally agreed that modern economic thought began with Adam Smith and his 1776 magnum opus, *An Inquiry into the Nature and Causes of the Wealth of Nations*. Smith, who was actually a philosopher—the economist profession didn't exist during his time—laid the foundational elements of the school of thought that has come to be known as Classical economics. According to the Classical school, the economy operates best when markets are mostly left to their own devices; in other words, when the government employs a laissez-faire, or hands-off, approach. The Classical school promoted the idea that prices (also known as the price mechanism) allocate resources efficiently, as if all economic activity were being guided by an **invisible hand**. The Classical school also advocated free trade, specialization, and the division of labor. The Classicals believed that wide-scale unemployment was a problem that would eventually correct itself as markets, left on their own to operate through the price mechanism, automatically moved the economy toward full employment. Therefore, in the Classical view, there was little or no role for the government in managing the economy. Adam Smith was the first of the Classical economists, but he wasn't the last. Other well-known economists associated with the Classical school include Thomas Malthus, David Ricardo, Jean-Baptiste Say, and John Stuart Mill.

The Marxist School

Marxism is as much a political philosophy as it is a school of economic thought. *The Communist Manifesto*, published in 1848 by Karl Marx and Friedrich Engels, lays out some of the authors' criticisms of capitalism. It contends that capitalism will one day be replaced by socialism and then, later on, by communism. The Marxist school focuses on the struggle

Adam Smith, the first of the Classical economists, is credited as the father of modern economic thought. (Opposite) Karl Marx's belief that workers must take ownership of the means of production inspired revolutions and labor movements throughout the world.

between the *bourgeoisie* (the capitalists or owners of the means of production) and the *proletariat* (the working class). The labor theory of value is a major component of Marxist economic thought. It states that the value of a good derives from the labor required to produce it. Marx didn't originate that idea—it actually appears in the writings of various Classical economists—but he did appropriate it and use it as an argument against capitalist profits. In his 1867 work *Capital: Critique of Political Economy*, Marx continued his criticism of the capitalist system by arguing that it's built entirely upon the exploitation of labor. Marx argued for the necessity of a socialist revolution that would establish what he called a "dictatorship of the proletariat." The ultimate goal, in the Marxist view, is public ownership of the means of production, distribution, and exchange. People sometimes think of Marxist economics as being diametrically opposed to Classical economics, and in a sense that's true. The Classicals advocated free markets, and Marxists favor the notion of tightly controlled markets or no markets at all (the grand vision of communism features a utopian society without money, and thus without trade). Clearly, the Marxist school has been influential in several places around the world, but much less so since the fall of the former Soviet Union.

The Neoclassical School

The Neoclassical school, whose ideas began to appear around 1870, built on the propositions of Classical economics and began to focus on some of the finer details of interactions in markets. The Neoclassical view begins with the assumption that people are basically rational when they make decisions. Neoclassicals believe that consumers behave rationally and attempt to maximize their utility, or satisfaction, within the limits of their available resources. Sellers, also assumed to be acting rationally, are seen as attempting to maximize their profits. The interaction between consumer demand and seller supply determines market prices. The focus on comparing additional costs and additional benefits, or **marginal analysis** (see page 36) also emerged from the Neoclassical school. Many of the economic fundamentals taught today are Neoclassical theories and approaches. Even the supply and demand curves prominently scrawled on college blackboards around the world came out of the Neoclassical movement.

The Keynesian School

In some respects, it isn't Marxism that represents the antithesis of the Classical view, but rather the school named after John Maynard Keynes (pronounced "*Kanes*"). The man behind the Keynesian school was no Marxist. He agreed with a number of basic tenets of Classical economics, such as the importance of the price mechanism. But he also disagreed with certain Classical ideas such as the notion that unemployment is self-correcting, or the belief that government has no significant role to play in correcting the economic problems of a nation, state, or region. Rather, Keynes and his disciples believed that government has the means, as well as the moral obligation, to counteract problems such as unemployment and inflation through its taxing and spending policies. Keynesian theories were first put into practice by President Franklin D. Roosevelt during the Great Depression, and they are among the most influential economic ideas to have emerged in the 20th century. Many present-day economists disagree with parts of the Keynesian view, but it still carries significant weight in Washington and other capitals around the world.

The Austrian School

The Austrian school of economic thought is related to the Neoclassical school and sometimes even seen as a subcomponent of that school. Many regard Carl Menger as the founder of the Austrian school. Other prominent economists from this school are Ludwig von Mises, Murray Rothbard, and Friedrich Hayek. While the Austrian view is, politically speaking, most closely aligned with the platform of the Libertarian Party, which emerged in Colorado in the early 1970s, it is in fact based not so much on political ideology as it is on economic analysis. As believers in and defenders of free markets, the Austrians are vehemently opposed to government involvement in the economy. Some people see the Austrian school as a fringe element of economic thought, but several of the school's adherents have contributed ideas to the mainstream. Hayek, for example, who wrote

the well-known book *The Road to Serfdom*, was co-awarded the Nobel Prize in Economics in 1974.

The New Institutional School

The New Institutional school of economic thought is another extension of Neoclassical economics. This school began to gain prominence in the latter part of the 20th century. New Institutional economics focuses on the role that legal and social norms, or institutions, play in the economy. One important idea that emerged from New Institutional economics is the concept of transaction costs, or the extra costs involved in the completion of a transaction. These include the costs associated with searching for products, negotiating terms, and enforcing agreements. Four Nobel laureates have been associated with the New Institutional school, the most famous being Ronald Coase, who believed, among other things, that real markets rather than theoretical ones were the appropriate purview of economic study.

The Monetarist School

Monetarism is another school of economic thought that argues for free markets. Monetarism applies to the macroeconomy and macroeconomic issues. It maintains that, in the short term, the economy's output, or gross domestic product (GDP), is primarily determined by the money supply, or the total amount of money in circulation. Over longer periods (or what economist typically refer to as "the long run") the key determinant of

the current-dollar GDP is the overall prices in the economy. Monetarists have been generally known to advocate a policy of steady money supply growth on the part of the Federal Reserve, which is drastically different from the Federal Reserve's policy of targeting interest rates. The Monetarist school was most prominent during the 1970s, when some important policymakers followed its prescriptions. Since that time, however, the school has fallen out of favor among economists in general, although some basic elements of Monetarism have made their way into mainstream economic thinking. Milton Friedman, a champion of Monetarism, was awarded the 1976 Nobel Prize in Economics. He was one of the economists who blamed Federal Reserve missteps for the severity of the Great Depression.

Economists disagree on how the government should regulate the economy. Monetarists, for example, believe the Fed should always seek to increase flow of cash.

The Behavioralist School

Behavioral economics, broadly speaking, borrows certain concepts and ideas from psychology and overlaps to some degree with that field. Behavioral economists disagree with the basic Neoclassical assumption that people are always rational decision makers. Through carefully designed laboratory experiments and other forms of research, behavioral economists have identified situations in which people are systematically irrational. Behavioral economics includes several different strands such as psychological economics, experimental economics, and behavioral finance. The field has provided some valuable insights into human behavior, and these have important implications for economic policy.

COMPARING THE SCHOOLS OF ECONOMIC THOUGHT

	Date of Origin	Key Figures	FOR
Classical	1776	• David Ricardo • John Stuart Mill • Jean-Baptiste Say • Adam Smith	• The "invisible hand" • Free markets • Laissez-faire ideas • Say's Law
Marxist	1848	• Friedrich Engels • Karl Marx	• Labor class • Intervention in the market
Neoclassical	1870	• William Jevons	• Laissez-faire approach to policy • Rational expectations • General equilibrium theory
Keynesian	1930s	• John Maynard Keynes	• Government intervention • Aggregate demand driving the economy
Austrian	1871	• Friedrich Hayek • Carl Menger • Ludvig von Mises • Murray Rothbard	• Free markets • Individual freedom • Unrestricted capitalism
Monetarist	1950s	• Milton Friedman	• Free markets • Policies of steady money growth
New Institutional	Late 20th century	• Ronald Coase • Douglass North • Oliver Williamson	• Transaction cost • Social norms affect human rationality
Behavorialist	1940s	• George Katona • Herbert Simon • Amos Tversky	• Understanding human biases • Prospect theory

	AGAINST	Premise	Political Associations
Classical	Outside intervention and mercantilism	The invisible hand of the free market is self-correcting and all we need to achieve equilibrium.	Conservatives
Marxist	Capitalist class power and inequality	Capitalism is imperfect, self-destructive, and requires outside intervention. The capitalist class will obtain exceptional power over the working class, resulting in massive inequality.	Communists, socialists, and liberals
Neoclassical	Assumptions based on irrational human behavior	Economic agents act rationally to maximize their utility and profits.	Mostly conservative, but no specific association to any party
Keynesian	Economists who argue that the government does not help capitalism	With active government intervention, business cycles can be managed through fiscal and monetary policies.	Appeals to some conservatives, but more so to liberals and moderates
Austrian	Government intervention	Free market can sustain itself and fix any economic problems. The economy will perform better with little or no government intervention.	Libertarians and conservatives
Monetarist	The gold standard	Government's role is to control inflation by controlling the money supply.	Mostly conservative, but no specific association to any party
New Institutional	Looking only at production cost	Institutions, or social and legal norms, influence economic activities.	No specific political associations
Behavorialist	The Neoclassical assumption that people are rational decision makers	It's important to study the way the human mind reacts and adapts to the markets and economy.	No specific political associations

1776

Invisible Hand
CLASSICAL

Scottish economist Adam Smith publishes *An Inquiry into the Nature and Causes of the Wealth of Nations*, in which he describes his theory of the free market as being guided by an "invisible hand."

1848

The Communist Manifesto
MARXIST

Karl Marx (above) and Friedrich Engels publish *The Communist Manifesto*, asserting that capitalism could lead only to a worker's revolution.

1871

Laissez-Faire Economics
AUSTRIAN

Carl Menger, widely regarded as the father of Austrian school, publishes *Principles of Economics*. His work asserts that people act rationally in terms of their self-interest, therefore justifying "laissez-faire" economics.

1817

Comparative Advantage
CLASSICAL

David Ricardo arrived at a number of important economic theories, including the theory of comparative advantage, which advocates free trade and the specialization of labor.

1871

Marginal Utility
NEOCLASSICAL

William Jevons describes the marginal utility theory of value, which looks at the diminishing satisfaction buyers gain from consuming additional units of a good.

1899

Conspicuous Consumption
INSTITUTIONAL

In *The Theory of the Leisure Class*, Thorstein Veblen coins the term "conspicuous consumption," or the way that people in capitalist societies frequently attempt to "one-up" each other with the accumulation of more products.

1936

Animal Spirits
KEYNESIAN

John Maynard Keynes uses the term "animal spirits" to describe the confidence that drives so many consumers to their spending decisions.

1944

Nash Equilibrium Theory
BEHAVIORALIST

The Nash Equilibrium theory is developed by John von Neumann and Oskar Morgenstern in *The Theory of Games and Economic Behavior*, a concept in game theory where even after considering the moves of their opponent, no one player has any incentive to change or deviate from their strategy.

1957

Bounded Rationality
BEHAVIORALIST

Nobel Economics laureate Herbert Simon develops the concept of bounded rationality, or the idea that human decision making is limited by the available information, cognitive load, and time to make a decision—resulting in a choice that may not be the most optimal.

1937

Transaction Costs
NEW INSTITUTIONAL

Ronald Coase points out transaction costs, or the expenses or budget of a firm, as an important factor in developing a firm's productivity. Without them, Coase notes, a company would be unable to efficiently plan their economic output.

1956

Money Matters
MONETARIST

To challenge John Maynard Keynes, Milton Friedman publishes *The Quantity Theory of Money*, which aims to show that the amount of money in the economy has a predictable effect on income.

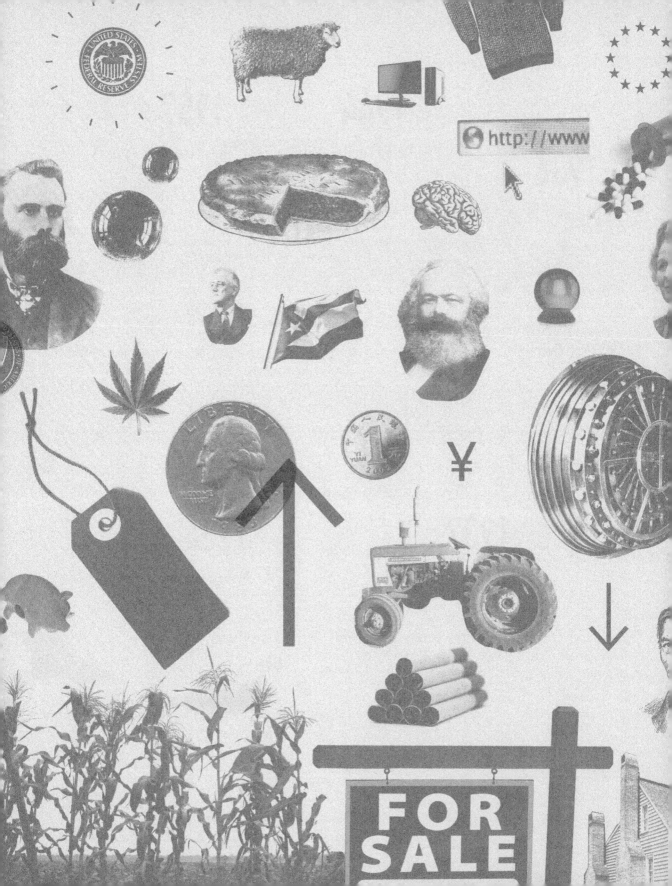

2 THINKING LIKE AN ECONOMIST

Economists see life a bit differently than most people. It's hard to know whether economists are born or made. Some economic thinking coincides with what many people call "common sense." But other theories, principles, and findings from the field of economics strike the average person as counterintuitive. This chapter introduces a few of the field's foundational elements. Several of the concepts covered address the reasons why consumers and sellers behave the way they do, and will help you see how economics and human behavior are inextricably linked. Although you may not be thinking totally like an economist by the end of the chapter, you'll hopefully gain some understanding about why economists see the world the way they do and why that's actually a good thing.

FUNDAMENTAL ECONOMIC CONCEPTS

In this section of the chapter, we'll take a look at incentives—what they are and why they matter. We'll also discuss different kinds of costs and how to think about them. Finally, we'll see how an economist understands the way people behave and whether people's behavior is rational or riddled with contradictions and biases.

Incentives

If you study enough economics, whether formally or informally, one idea you're sure to walk away with is the notion of an **incentive**. The idea that incentives matter is more a fact of life than an economic theory, but it does show up fairly often in economics. That's because economists tend to think about incentives more often than most other people.

Incentives do appear in our daily lives. For example, when a company offers its sales personnel bonuses for surpassing their sales quotas, the company is employing the basic idea of incentives. To take another example, a government's policymakers use incentives when they attempt to influence people's behavior; so-called "sin taxes" on cigarettes and alcohol are intended to encourage consumers to cut down on their use of these potentially harmful products.

Incentives can be very effective when they're carefully constructed, but plenty of well-intentioned incentives have ended up being governed by the *law of unintended consequences* or have even completely backfired. (To be clear, this law is less a principle of economics than it is a commonly accepted fact of life.) A moment ago we looked at one type of incentive in the government sector. Consider now an example from the private sector—namely, the National Football League (NFL)—involving

Ken O'Brien, formerly a quarterback for the New York Jets. Early in his career with the team, O'Brien threw more interceptions than the team's management could tolerate. (For those of you who are not football fans, this means that often when O'Brien attempted to throw the football to a teammate, the ball was caught, or intercepted, by a player for the opposing team.) To solve this problem, the Jets offered O'Brien what you might call a negative incentive—a clause was added into O'Brien's contract to specify that he would be penalized for each interception he threw. The solution worked, at least in the sense that O'Brien threw fewer interceptions, as expected. The unintended consequence, however, was that he avoided throwing the football.

Now let's turn again to the government sector. Some people argue that certain environmental regulations actually end up harming the environment. One of the best-known examples of this argument is the Endangered Species Act. In theory, the intent of the act has been to protect certain species of animals that the government deems threatened or endangered. But stories abound of landowners who have intentionally modified their land (e.g., cutting down trees) to render it inhospitable as a habitat for the very species that the act seeks to protect. Some landowners

IF THE SHOE DOESN'T FIT

This true story comes from Poland. It's about a government-owned shoe factory in the days when the country had a much more socialist economy, and it's a great instance of how incentives affect behavior.

Every month, the Polish government allotted the factory materials, and the manager was told to produce a fixed number of shoes. Because there was no profit motive involved, the manager's basic goal was to meet the quota in the easiest possible way—by producing only small shoes.

As you might expect, this production strategy created a problem for Polish people who had big feet, and so the government overhauled the system. Now the factory received the same allotment of materials, but instead of producing a fixed number of shoes, the factory was expected to produce a fixed number of *tons* of shoes. In other words, the factory's production, or output, would now be weighed rather than counted. You can probably guess the result: The factory's manager responded in the most efficient way, by producing nothing but shoes the size of gunboats.

In either situation, the manager was incentivized to complete the quota of shoes in the fastest way possible. The government's strategy did not provide any motivation to produce shoes in a variety of sizes that accommodated people's needs.

(Opposite) Though meant to curb harmful behavior, "sin taxes" may also unintentionally create a market for cheaper products "smuggled" from states with lower taxes.

are also said to have eradicated protected species as soon as they were spotted on the land, before the endangered animals had a chance to reproduce, increase their numbers, and create a regulatory headache.

Consider what happened in the wake of the 2007–2008 financial crisis, when the federal government bailed out a number of large banks and other financial institutions. When the government bails out one large financial institution, it also creates an incentive for other large financial institutions to behave less responsibly. Why should the managers of a big bank be careful and take appropriate actions to manage their risk? After all, if they get into trouble, won't the government just bail them out? Why should a bank that was bailed out in the past behave responsibly in the future? If it was too big to fail before, it will be too big to fail in the future, too.

Although the idea that incentives matter may seem obvious, a lot of smart people are unclear on the concept. But actions have consequences. For example, if a city government doubles its sales tax rate, citizens will react. Some will reduce their consumption of taxed goods. Others will shop in a neighboring town. If the tax hike is burdensome enough, still others may move away. In each case, the

Critics of the 2008 Troubled Asset Relief Program, which dedicated hundreds of billions of dollars to "bailing out" Wall Street, say it took away incentives for financial responsibility.

tax increase had the unintended consequence of lowering the city's tax base.

Rules and operating procedures are a necessary component of responsible governing. But government policymakers and business managers who are thinking about implementing a new measure should make sure they've considered the potential changes in incentive structures. If they fail to think the issue through, they'll learn about the unintended consequences the hard way.

Opportunity Costs

Another fundamental in economics is the concept of **opportunity costs.** This concept separates the economists from the accountants. When an accountant looks at the costs involved in an enterprise, she records out-of-pocket costs like wages, utilities, and similar expenses in her ledger. But if the accountant were an economist, she would consider not just those types of explicit costs, but also the *implicit* costs involved in the enterprise. In other words, she would take the opportunity costs into account.

So what is an opportunity cost? It's when a choice has to be made between two or more alternatives, and only one of the alternatives can be chosen. In other words, choosing one alternative means forgoing the opportunity to enjoy the benefits of the best alternative that *isn't* chosen. Should a firm close its Sheboygan plant or its Walla Walla plant? Which of two important federal programs should have its funding increased? Should you study for your chemistry exam or go out partying with your friends? A situation may present more than two options, of course; in fact, there may be thousands of options from which to choose. But in any situation where only *one* option can be chosen, the forfeited value of the best option that is *not* chosen is the cost of that choice—its opportunity cost.

Suppose that your favorite possession is your flat-screen television, and that your second favorite possession is your laptop computer. Now imagine (heaven forbid) that a fire breaks out in the room where you keep these items. As the smoke begins to thicken, you realize that you can save only one of them. If you save your TV, then the opportunity cost of your decision is your computer. If you save your computer, then the opportunity cost is your TV.

This concept works the same way in business. A company's expansion into 10 new regions means that expansion into other areas has to wait. If only one employee can be promoted to vice president, then the company forgoes the opportunity to use the second best candidate's skill set in that position. A new product's development pulls resources away from the existing product line. A choice has to be made, of course, but it's good business for the company to consider what it will mean to forgo the value of the next best alternative—that is, what the opportunity cost will be—before investing serious time or money into any project or decision.

Opportunity costs aren't always easy to quantify, however. If two college students choose to enroll in a particular class instead of enrolling in other classes, then each of them incurs an opportunity cost. However, the opportunity cost of enrolling in that particular class won't be the same for both of them. And individually, the opportunity cost may not be the same from day to day. For example, if one of the students gives up the chance to work an extra shift so he can attend class, then his opportunity cost is easily quantifiable—it's equal to the amount of money he would have earned if he'd skipped class and worked the extra shift. But what if his second best option was taking a nap? It's not easy to place a dollar value on a nap, but if anyone can do it, it's an economist, as we're about to see.

Cost-Benefit Analysis

Economists are experts in assigning monetary value to things that don't ordinarily have dollar signs attached to them. Chief among these experts are economists who specialize in performing what is known as **cost-benefit analysis**. As the term implies, cost-benefit analysis involves comparing the cost of a given action with the benefit (value) of that action.

For example, if a transportation department wants to install barriers along the median of a busy highway, then the department

Economic tools like cost-benefit analyses play into public policy when governments have to calculate funding for road safety projects.

may hire an economist to perform a cost-benefit analysis of the proposed installation. The costs—material, labor, and overhead—will be relatively easy to calculate. But figuring out the benefit of the project will be trickier. That's not because information is lacking. The transportation department knows how many accidents occur every year along the highway, how many of those accidents involve cars crossing the median, and how many fatalities result. Barrier manufacturers and vendors know how effective the barriers are, and so do highway officials in other states that have erected similar barriers. This information can help the transportation department estimate the number of lives saved if the barriers are installed. The tricky part is assigning a dollar value to each saved life and then directly comparing the total cost of the barriers to the total value of the lives likely to be saved.

Every life is precious, of course, but we don't have infinite resources for saving one life, cold and uncaring though that fact may sound. We could build barriers along every stretch of road in the country, and in the end a single precious life might be saved, and that would be wonderful. But if we did that, we wouldn't have anything left to spend on schools, or healthcare, or national defense.

Yet who can possibly place a dollar value on a human life? An economist, that's who. That value is somewhere between $6 million and $9 million, depending on the economist or government agency you ask.

MAN BITES CHILI DOG: A TASTE OF MARGINAL ANALYSIS

Along with cost-benefit analysis, economists often engage in **marginal analysis,** which has to do with comparing additional (marginal) benefits and costs. **Marginal cost** is any additional cost incurred by engaging in some activity, and **marginal benefit** is any additional benefit derived from engaging in that activity. According to economic theory (not to mention common sense), you should engage in an activity if its marginal benefit to you will be greater than its marginal cost. Conversely, if the marginal cost will be greater than the marginal benefit, then you'd be crazy to engage in that activity.

Let's say Jack is standing in front of a hot dog stand. The price of a plain hot dog is $3, and the price of a chili dog is $4. If Jack thinks he'll get at least $4 worth of benefit from buying and consuming a $4 chili dog, then he should order one. In this case, the marginal cost of consuming one chili dog will be the $4 he forks over to the vendor. The marginal benefit will be harder to quantify, but it will essentially consist of whatever satisfaction Jack derives from the flavor of the chili dog and sating his hunger. His marginal benefit will be at least as great as his

marginal cost, which means he'll end up feeling that he got his money's worth, and maybe more. But if Jack has only $3 worth of appetite, then he should choose the plain $3 hot dog. If he were to order the $4 chili dog, his marginal cost would be $4, but he would gain only $3 worth of benefit. His marginal cost would be greater than his marginal benefit, and he'd end up feeling that he didn't get his money's worth.

Now let's suppose that Jack actually is hungry enough to order a $4 chili dog. In addition, he loves chili dogs so much that he knows this one will deliver $5 worth of benefit to him. But after he eats it, he's still somewhat hungry. Will the marginal benefit he derives from eating a second chili dog still be $5?

For most of us, the marginal benefit of that second chili dog would definitely be less, and so the second chili dog would be worth less than the first one. Here's the economic principle behind that reality: As we consume more and more units of a particular good over a given period of time, the benefit, or utility, we derive from that good tends to fall with each successive unit that we consume. This is the principle of **diminishing marginal benefit** or *diminishing marginal utility.* In economic theory, the optimal level of consumption occurs where marginal benefit equals marginal cost.

Therefore, if Jack has only $3 worth of appetite after eating the first chili dog, he shouldn't buy another one, since his marginal cost ($4) will be greater than his marginal benefit ($3). Instead, he can satisfy his remaining hunger (and derive a marginal benefit) by purchasing a plain $3 hot dog. Or better yet, Jack can arrive at his optimal level of chili dog consumption by negotiating with the vendor to buy a $3-size portion of a chili dog.

$3

$5

$4

Economists have also developed a number of methods for assigning dollar values to forests, rivers, clean air, and the like. When government officials think about protecting and preserving an old-growth forest, for example, they need to understand something about that forest's value. The timber in an old-growth forest has economic value. It can be sold to builders, paper manufacturers, and other parties.

But an economist will be interested in more than just the market value of the timber. An economist will consider the forest's value to hikers, as well as to local and visiting sightseers. An economist will also consider the forest's **nonuse value**, which is the value it holds for people who will never use the forest for any activity or harvest its trees for any purpose; they simply enjoy knowing that the old-growth forest is there, and that its trees are still standing.

By the same token, when a sports team wants a municipality to subsidize the construction of an expensive football stadium that will sit idle for much of the year, the team often hires an economist to produce a cost-benefit analysis, which typically includes some estimate of the team's nonuse value. The argument is that even though the local citizens themselves will never take the field and score touchdowns, or may never attend a game at all, they will still derive benefit, in the form of civic pride, from their city's association with a professional sports team. That's a fairly shaky argument, as we'll see in chapter 3 when we talk about the social costs and social benefits associated with different kinds of markets. Not every citizen cares about sports or associates civic pride with a sports team, but every citizen does pay for a publicly financed football stadium, and the facility's owners stand to benefit far more than its users.

Sunk Costs

Another type of cost, one that often confounds people, is **sunk cost**. A sunk cost has already been borne and can never be reclaimed or recovered. For example, when you purchase a nonrefundable airline ticket, you incur a sunk cost as soon as your payment goes through.

Most people have no trouble understanding what a sunk cost is, but people often react to sunk costs in ways that go against the recommendations of economic theory. Economic theory suggests that if a sunk cost you've already incurred constitutes one element of a decision that you're facing, you should ignore the sunk cost and focus instead on the costs and benefits you'll face as you go forward. Your attention should be on your future marginal costs and marginal benefits, not on your sunk costs. Sometimes people actually do ignore sunk costs, as economists advise, but in many situations they make sunk costs a very important part of their decision making.

Let's look at an example. Suppose you've spent $150 for a ticket to an upcoming concert. On the day of the concert, your car breaks down. Because of the petroleum crisis that began a few days after you bought your ticket, the price of gasoline has skyrocketed to $8 per gallon, and all the taxi companies have shut down. You'll have to rent a car if you want to attend the concert. On top of that, there's a prohibition against reselling tickets to this concert, and the prohibition is strictly enforced.

The car rental and the gas will cost you a total of $125, and you'll also have to pay $35 for parking. As it happens, on the day of the concert you also learn that you can stream the concert live online for a fee of $35. If you'd known about the online option in the first place, that's the option you might have chosen.

The sensible thing for you to do is stay home, pay $35, and stream the concert online. You'll be forfeiting the $150 you paid for your ticket, but that $150 is a sunk cost; you'll never get that money back. Since it doesn't matter to you whether you attend the concert in person or watch it live online, your marginal benefit will be essentially the same in either case. But your marginal cost—your *additional* cost—will be very different. To attend the concert in person, your marginal cost will be the $160 you'll pay to rent a car, park it, and fill the tank before you return it. If you watch the concert online, your marginal cost will be $35. The $35 option is the more sensible one.

Nevertheless, people in a situation like this one often become fixated on the money they've already spent, to the point where they see the earlier expenditure as requiring them to spend even more money. In other words, instead of ignoring their sunk costs, they incorporate their sunk costs into their decisions. To put this in a more familiar way, they throw good money after bad—and that's something an economist would never recommend.

Rational Behavior and Types of Preferences

A big part of economics involves studying patterns of decision making. The field of economics, throughout much of its history, has operated on the core assumption that most people, most of the time, exhibit *rational behavior* in their decision-making processes. After all, a science built around decision-making behavior has to assume that people usually make decisions in certain, predictable ways. Assuming rational behavior also means that an economist will see people as generally making choices that will produce the most benefit to themselves.

Let's consider Ellen, who says she has no preference between Coca-Cola and Pepsi. She walks into a convenience store and sees a can of Coca-Cola and a can of Pepsi sitting side by side. Each can contains 12 ounces of soda, both have the same expiration date, and neither is dented or degraded in any way. The can of Coca-Cola costs $1 and the can of Pepsi costs $0.75. An economist will assume that Ellen will choose the Pepsi if she's a rational decision maker—it's in her best interest to buy the cheaper soda and pocket the difference of $0.25. But suppose she chooses the Coca-Cola. Is she being irrational? Not necessarily. Maybe when Ellen said she had no preference between the two brands of cola, she simply wasn't telling the truth. That doesn't have to mean she's a liar; maybe she didn't become aware of her actual preference until she actively had to choose. In fact, there's often a gap between what people say they like (*stated preferences*) and the preferences they express when forced to make a real choice (*revealed preferences*). That's one reason why a dozen political polls can sometimes all predict the wrong outcome—some candidates are easy to support in theory, but hearts and minds can suddenly change in the voting booth.

There's also the ordering of preferences. Consider Ted, who is shopping for a current-year Toyota Prius. He's somewhat open when it comes to the car's color, but his first choice is black, followed by gray, and then red. When Ted pulls into the dealer's lot, the salesman shows him two current-year models that have the same price tag and are identical in every way but color—one is black and the other is red. In this situation, Ted can be expected to choose the black car. If he's asked to choose between a gray model and a red one, he can be expected to choose the gray model. When Ted's choices reflect the order of his conscious preferences, Ted is exhibiting *transitive preferences*, which are assumed to underlie rational decision making. But if Ted were to choose a red Prius over a gray one, or a gray Prius over a black one, then he could not be said to be exhibiting transitive preferences. In fact, an economist might say that Ted was not being rational. (Incidentally, economists have

conducted experiments showing that children are much less likely than adults to exhibit transitive preferences; for this reason, children are not always rational in their decision making and may need help from adults.)

Purposeful Behavior, Bounded Rationality, Behavioral Economics, and Biases

Even if people don't always exhibit rational behavior, an economist sees people as always exhibiting at least some type and degree of *purposeful behavior*, which means having some outcome in mind. An outcome may be based on rational reasoning, reasoning filtered through one or more biases, emotional reasoning, or it may be tied to nothing but sheer impulse.

We don't always know exactly how we reached a particular decision. We just know that the outcome feels good. Maybe we didn't have all the information we needed during the decision process. Maybe we didn't have time to analyze all the variables. We simply made the best decision we could with the information we had, and in the time that was available. Our thinking wasn't irrational. It was actually quite practical, and it was the type of decision process that crops up quite often, whether we're at work or making a choice that will affect us more personally. Our process was rational within certain limits, and an economist would see it as an example of *bounded rationality*.

One particular subfield of economics, **behavioral economics**, has shed light on situations in which people are, so to speak, predictably irrational. For example, how a piece of information is framed influences the way it is perceived. Let's say your boss gives you a $500 bonus after you've spent a few months at your new job. You're thrilled, but then you find out that your colleague, who started the same day you did, got a bonus of $2,000. Now your gain looks to you like a loss. This is what economists call the **framing effect**. Marketers know all about this one—the manufacturer of a new medical device claims that it's effective for 90 percent of patients but never mentions the 10 percent who aren't helped at all, or a health insurer touts a plan that costs only $10 a day (which sounds better than $300 per month). Behavioral economics also has a lot to say about certain tendencies that affect decision making and are known collectively as **cognitive biases**.

YOU SCREAM, I SCREAM . . . TOO MANY ASSUMPTIONS?

Economists are often criticized for making too many assumptions, but without assumptions there would be no economic models, and our knowledge of economics would be very limited.

Since just about every situation can be improved by the presence of ice cream, let's use the following example to find out why assumptions are not only necessary in economics but also helpful in developing new economic insights.

Suppose you own an ice cream store and want to find out whether your advertising budget is having any effect on your sales. You decide to conduct an experiment: For two months, you're going to carefully record your sales. During the first month, you'll keep your advertising budget at $1,000. During the second month, you'll raise it to $2,000. At the end of the second month, you'll compare your sales for the first and second months. Then you'll know how your advertising expenditures are affecting sales, right?

No, sorry.

Your advertising expenditures are not the only factor that may be influencing your sales. There's the quality of your service and product, and, of course, your prices.

All right, then. What if you not only doubled your advertising budget during the second month but also cut your prices in half? Would you sell more ice cream? Absolutely. Would you learn more about how your advertising budget affects your sales? Absolutely not, because you would have wrecked your experiment by changing too many variables.

To conduct a valid experiment, you would have to raise your advertising budget while keeping everything else the same—the quality of your service, the quality of your product, and your prices. By carrying out the experiment in this way, you would be using the basic assumption of **ceteris paribus** (see page 45), and you would probably end up with some helpful data that could guide your advertising expenditures.

- **Gambler's Fallacy.** This is familiar to anyone who gambles or knows a gambler. If you flip a coin nine times in a row and it comes up heads each time, you may believe that the coin will surely come up tails on the next flip, and you may even be willing to bet big money on that outcome. From a statistical standpoint, however, the coin is just as likely to come up heads as tails on the next flip. That's because each flip of the coin is an independent event. And if you think **gambler's fallacy** is exclusive to casinos and Friday night poker, you're not paying attention to the stock market.

- **Confirmation Bias.** People have a tendency to seek out information that they already agree with. If you're supporting a political candidate, for example, you may tend to notice (and pass on to others) nothing but positive news about your candidate even though there's plenty of negative news, too. We know what we want, we know what we like, and **confirmation bias** sends us out into the world, physically or virtually, in search of exactly those things.

- **Anchoring Effect.** The **anchoring effect** comes up in many decision-making contexts where people exhibit a tendency to lock on to the first piece of information they receive. In a price negotiation, for example, the buyer or the seller may begin by stating a certain price, and then every

Some of the rules of the casino, like the gambler's fallacy, also apply to the investment habits of high-stakes Wall Street players.

subsequent counterbid is compared to that price. Or a customer could walk into a store, see an item on sale, and not help but compare the sale price to the original price, which is often prominently displayed so the retailer can take advantage of the anchoring effect.

- **Status Quo Bias.** The **status quo bias** is the tendency to preserve the current state of affairs. A good example of this bias can be found in people's behavior around employer-sponsored retirement plans, the 401(k) and individual retirement accounts (IRAS) that have largely replaced the pensions of the past. When such plans were new, employees had to opt in, or specifically state that they wanted to participate. Later on, employees were automatically enrolled in the plans and had to opt out if they didn't want to participate. What does this have to do with the status quo bias? Simply this: Participation in the plans was found to rise significantly when employees were automatically enrolled and had to opt out, versus when they were offered the opportunity to enroll and had to opt in. If decision making was always rational, an employee would make the same choice about participating (or not participating) whether it was necessary to opt in or opt out. The status quo bias carries

considerable weight in human decision making, and employers took advantage of the status quo bias to promote retirement savings through automatic enrollment in retirement plans.

- **Endowment Effect.** The human tendency to stick with the status quo is the power behind the bias known as the **endowment effect** (in fact, the endowment effect is often seen as the status quo bias by another name). People under the influence of this cognitive bias place more value on goods if they happen to own them than they would if they didn't own those goods. For example, if your neighbor owns a piece of land and you ask her what she's willing to sell it for, she may say $250,000. However, if she didn't own the land and you asked her what she'd be willing to pay for it, she might say $100,000. In a completely rational world, the land would have the same value regardless of who owned it. Because of the endowment effect, however, many potential market transactions never take place. How can they, if sellers believe that the value of their goods is higher than buyers judge it to be?

(Opposite) The "endowment effect" is a behavioral bias on the part of sellers that may ultimately distort the market price of a good such as real estate.

FUNDAMENTAL ECONOMIC MODELS AND ASSUMPTIONS

So far in this chapter, we've been discussing basic economic concepts, but if you want to think like an economist, you need to know about basic economic models and assumptions, too. We've already looked at a few assumptions used by economists, including the most fundamental assumption that most people, most of the time, act rationally when they make decisions. In this section, we'll explore some assumptions that are specifically related to economic models.

A model, of course, is a small-scale version of something bigger. A model train looks like a real train, and it may even run like a real train, but everyone knows it's not even close to being a real train. In the same way, an economist's model of the economy and its various aspects is a small-scale version that can't hope to capture everything going on in the actual economy. The economy is a huge system with lots of simultaneously moving parts. It would be difficult for us to learn anything about the economy or the field of economics if we tried to take it all in at once, so models let us focus on specific features and isolate particular effects.

SHOULD THE GOVERNMENT NUDGE PEOPLE TO MAKE BETTER DECISIONS?

As behavioral economists and psychologists have demonstrated, people are predictably irrational in certain contexts. Should that fact be used to benefit people? For example, we know (from experiments and general observation) that people at a buffet tend to choose healthier dishes if salad is placed at the beginning of the food line. Wouldn't it therefore be advantageous to encourage people to eat better by arranging the food in that manner? In the case of employer-sponsored retirement plans, isn't it a good thing for employers to take advantage of the **status quo bias** (see page 42), force employees to opt out, and thus maximize retirement savings? If employers should leverage human irrationality in the interest of better decisions, then what about the government?

Some policymakers and economists certainly believe that this is a proper role for government. President Obama brought in an expert on the matter, Cass Sunstein, to be the administrator of the Office of Information and Regulatory Affairs. For the period of time he served, Sunstein oversaw an effort to develop policies that would nudge citizens into making better decisions. Likewise, UK Prime Minister David Cameron established a Behavioural Insights Team (BIT) for the purpose of setting up helpful nudges. In one of its initiatives, the BIT placed an additional line of text in letters sent out to taxpayers simply stating, "Most people pay their taxes on time." This subtle reminder resulted in drastically fewer late payments.

Governments see this type of nudging as benevolent—good for individuals and ultimately for society. However, not everyone is thrilled with the idea of the government encouraging certain types of behavior and discouraging others, however subtly. Libertarian-leaning individuals in particular find the practice manipulative, offensive, and somewhat Orwellian. Some feel that it's an example of the government overstepping its bounds and becoming a quasi-parent ("Eat more broccoli and skip the chocolate cake").

Wherever you come down on the question of nudges from the government, you have to acknowledge that government has learned its tactics from the experts—the many businesses that use advertising to nudge their customers into buying more of their products.

Many (though not all) economic **fore-casting models** assume that future events are more or less predictable based on events that have already occurred. For example, a model designed to predict next quarter's unemployment rate will be built on the assumption that the basic structure of the economy won't change before the next quarter. That's a sound assumption most of the time. If something completely unforeseen takes place—say, the collapse of the country's central government—then the forecast is likely to be wrong because of the faulty assumption at its base. Economic forecasting models are still useful, however, even though unforeseen events can and sometimes do prove their basic assumptions false.

Every economic model has to start from some type of assumption. A given model may incorporate its own particular set of assumptions, but some assumptions tend to be common to a variety of economic models.

Every economic model starts with at least some kind of *generalization*. If you want to build a model that predicts consumers' behavior, then you might build it on the assumption that all consumers are influenced by a general set of similar preferences. You may decide to make your model more complex by building in the assumption that consumers have different types of preferences, but you might also make the assumption that those differences can all be accounted for by five or six general categories. (In fact, your model would be unwieldy if you didn't make that assumption.) In other words, some economic models are quite complex and contain vast amounts of detailed data, but they all use simplifying generalizations.

Another assumption commonly used in economic models is that of **ceteris paribus,** which is Latin for "all other things being equal." In any economic analysis, there's some factor of primary interest. For example, in a model intended to forecast the price of gasoline in the next quarter, the factor of interest might be the price of gasoline. Yet a number of other factors, or variables, can affect the future price of gasoline. When economists employ the *ceteris paribus* assumption, they are assuming that those variables (such as political events affecting the ability to drill for oil) can be held constant while the primary item of interest is being analyzed.

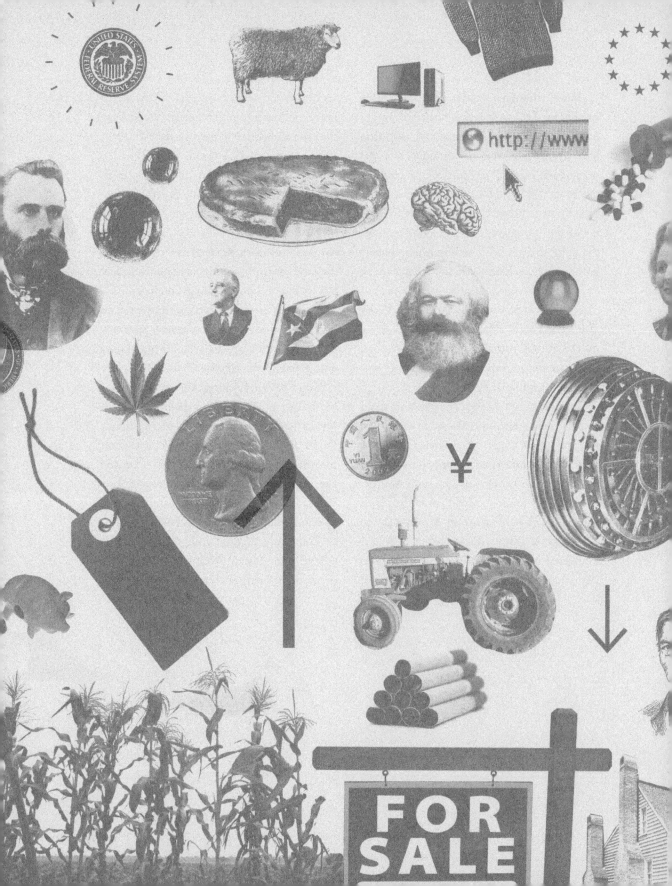

FOR
SALE

3 FREE MARKETS VERSUS GOVERNMENT REGULATION

One of the great political debates of our day centers on the question of how large the government should be. Where economics is concerned, the question has to do with when the government should intervene in a particular market, and when the market should be allowed to operate freely. Some politicians and pundits pride themselves on being champions of the free market, but most people (other than extreme libertarians) would agree that regulation is useful in some situations. This chapter provides an overview of markets and how they operate, as well as what happens when they don't work the way they're supposed to. The chapter also lays out the economic case for certain types of regulation. A few specific markets and forms of government intervention are discussed, including rent controls, agricultural price supports, the minimum wage, and the market for legal marijuana.

THE MIRACLE OF MARKETS

Markets are nothing short of miraculous. No computer, and certainly no human being or group of human beings, could track and coordinate all the activity necessary to make commerce run as smoothly as it does in free markets. You could say that markets are one of humanity's most amazing inventions—but that wouldn't be quite accurate. A free market is truly amazing, and yet it's not exactly an invention. It's simply a form of human interaction, a means for people to express their tastes, have their wants and needs met, and earn their livelihoods by serving their fellow human beings.

Some commentators would have you believe that markets were created by modern corporations, but markets were around long before corporations came into being. (Unlike markets, the corporation *is* a human invention.) If all the corporations in the world were

abolished tomorrow, markets would still exist, and they would still thrive.

Other people believe that markets were created by politicians, particularly politicians with a pro-business slant, but there are plenty of markets that exist outside politics—and outside the law, for that matter. Some markets persist in the face of laws designed to shut them down. If every politician fell off the planet next week, and if every law on the books were overturned, markets would survive.

What, then, is meant by the term *market*? A **market** is an institution or medium that connects potential buyers with potential sellers. When economists discuss markets, they're often referring to markets for particular goods or services. This means that the term *market* can refer to something broad, as well as something narrow. For example, the market for sports entertainment is fairly broad, but we could narrow the discussion by focusing on the market for Major League Baseball games, and we could narrow it even more by focusing on the market for tickets to games played by the New York Yankees, or on the market for tickets to a Yankees game to be played on a given night.

No matter how narrow and specific an individual market may be, it contains and is affected by all the forces that come into play in every market that is allowed to operate freely. Those forces include the interaction between the level of demand for a particular good or service, and the available supply of that good or service, with prices serving as a signal for buyers and sellers alike.

Demand is simply the consumer's need or desire for a good or a service. If the price of a New York Yankees ticket is $50, consumers may express demand for a total of 50,000 tickets. If the price of a ticket falls to $25, then consumers may express demand for a total of 80,000 tickets. When the price of a good falls, people are generally willing and able to buy more of the good. When the price rises, people are generally willing and able to buy less of the good. This basic notion—that people tend to want more of a good at a lower price and less of the good at a higher price—is embodied in a fundamental principle in economics known as the **law of demand**. For the law of demand to work, the assumption of *ceteris paribus* (see page 45) must come into play. For example, if the price of New York Yankees tickets were to fall, consumers might be willing to buy more tickets—but not if they learned that the price had fallen because of management's decision to bench the actual Yankees for the entire season and field the Charleston RiverDogs, a Yankees farm team, instead.

On the seller's side of things, the forces of supply are at work. Suppose that the Zipp Shoe Company is willing to provide the market with one million pairs of its shoes priced at $100 each, and with three million pairs priced

A 19th-century depiction of the Dock Street wharf in Philadelphia shows the everyday commotion of market interactions between sellers, buyers, and port workers.

at $200 each. In other words, the **law of supply** says that when the price of a good rises, sellers are willing to provide greater quantities of the good, and that when the price falls, sellers are willing to provide less of the good. Once again, the law can't work without the assumption of *ceteris paribus*. If the company believes it can sell its shoes for $200 a pair, then the company may be willing to put three million pairs of its shoes on the market—but not if the company has reason to suspect that a deep recession is on the way.

Demand and supply are not constant, however. In any market, many factors can affect the level of demand and the available supply for a good or service, including:

- When consumers' incomes go up, demand for most goods rises.

- When sellers' costs for raw materials go down, sellers are able to supply more of their products without raising prices.

- Business taxes can affect the supply of goods and services, and so can subsidies.

- Demand for something (such as conventional taxi service) is affected when a substitute (such as Uber) enters the market, and prices are affected as well.

The laws of supply and demand are central to determining prices and availability of goods. The point where both factors meet is known as the "market equilibrium."

Factors like these cause demand and supply to shift and move. Demand and supply gravitate toward a point, called the **equilibrium**, where the quantity of a good that sellers are willing to provide is the same as the quantity of the good that consumers want to purchase. Out of that interaction emerges the **market price**. Maybe you've heard sellers of products say that they charge the prices that the market will bear. What they mean is that they don't set their prices in a vacuum. Consumers, by expressing demand for products and services, have a lot to say about how much of a product or a service can be sold, and at what price. Julia is free to charge $1 million for handcrafted birdcages, but if no one wants to pay her price, she'll quickly find herself out of business.

Markets, left to themselves, are usually highly efficient; they allocate goods and services faster and with less waste than would be

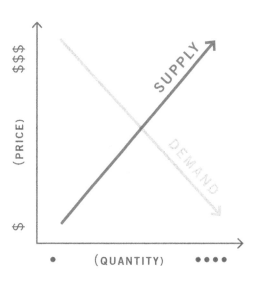

possible by any other means, such as central planning. If consumers want more chocolate bunnies, for example, then their demand for the long-eared confections will rise, and if nothing else changes (*ceteris paribus,* remember?), then the increased demand will push up the market price of chocolate bunnies. As the price begins to rise, several things will happen:

1. Some consumers will decide that they don't want to buy chocolate bunnies at the new, higher price, and those consumers will either save their money or spend it on something else, such as gummy worms.

2. Manufacturers of chocolate bunnies will notice that sellers are commanding higher prices for the luscious lagomorphs, and will correctly understand that the higher prices are a sign that consumers want more of the candy. They will ramp up production, and if the price of chocolate bunnies rises enough, new manufacturers may enter the market in search of profits.

3. As manufacturers make a greater supply of chocolate bunnies available for sellers to offer consumers, the price of the candy begins to come down, since chocolate bunnies are now so easy for buyers to find that sellers must compete with one another. And that's a good thing— wouldn't it be sad if some people couldn't afford their favorite treat because the price was too high?

Each time there's a change in the forces that underlie demand or supply, the market responds and a new equilibrium is reached. No individual or centralized agency coordinates any of this activity, and no one needs to. It occurs naturally as an outgrowth of human interaction.

MARKET FAILURE AND MARKET REGULATION

Markets are amazing and beautiful when they work well, and in most instances, they work very well indeed. When they don't, we have what economists refer to as **market failure,** a situation in which a market, left to its own devices, produces either more or less than the **socially optimal** amount of a good or a service.

Causes of Market Failure

Market failures arise most commonly because of poor or incomplete information, lack of competition, or the presence of external costs or benefits.

Poor or Incomplete Information

Sometimes the level of information in a market is poor or incomplete. Typically in such a case, one party to a transaction will have more information than the other party. In a situation like this one, economists say there is **asymmetric information**. Let's consider some examples.

- The seller of a used car knows more about the car's qualities than the potential buyer does. The buyer, lacking complete information about the car, won't be able to make a wise buying decision.

- In a country without labeling regulations, the manufacturers of a popular lunch meat are not required to disclose the product's ingredients, but buyers might not choose to purchase it at all if they knew everything it contained.

- A manufacturer of potato chips advertises its product as being "all natural" and low in fat, but in fact the chips are loaded with fat and unnatural ingredients.

Information asymmetries like these can lead to a market outcome that is less than socially optimal, such as the presence of unsafe cars on the road, the ingestion of non-human-grade meat scraps, and the consumption of products linked to obesity and heart disease. (Note that *market outcome* simply refers to the results of interactions between forces in a market.)

Lack of Competition

When market outcomes that are less than desirable can be traced to lack of competition, one of the following situations may be at the root of the problem:

- The market for a product or service is monopolized—that is, potential consumers have only one source of this product or service—which means that the product or service will have a higher price than it would if the same market were competitive, and the sales volume of the product or service will be lower than in a competitive market.

- The market is not monopolized, but it's still not competitive enough.

The outcome is not socially optimal in either of these scenarios, because the market fails to attract potential consumers who would be willing to buy the product or service if it were competitively priced.

External Costs and Benefits

When external costs or benefits—**externalities**—become a factor in market failure, it's because people who are not directly involved in a market transaction are nevertheless affected by it, sometimes negatively and sometimes positively. External *costs* are known as **negative externalities,** and external *benefits*, as you might suppose, are called **positive externalities**. Let's see what these two causes of market failure look like in practice.

- **Negative Externality.** A chemicals manufacturer has a factory next to a river where the company dumps its toxic waste. People living in a community two miles downstream get their drinking water from the river. None of them work at the factory, and none of them buy the company's products, which are shipped to industrial customers in distant cities.

In this case, a market transaction—the sale of chemicals—generates an external cost, or negative externality, that is borne by the neighboring community. This is a market failure because the company is overproducing chemicals. How do we know this? We know it because the company is avoiding the monetary costs involved in responsible disposal of its toxic waste and is passing those costs on to its neighbors, in the form of environmental pollution and risks to their health. If the company were forced to internalize those external costs—that is, if the company had to pay those costs instead of passing them on to its downstream neighbors—then the company would also have to try to recover those costs by raising the market price of its chemicals, and the volume of its sales would drop.

Environmental pollution is considered an external cost of production because of its impact on the surrounding community, and it can also be seen as a market failure.

- **Positive Externality.** Dan and Fred carpool to work every day. As winter approaches, Dan gets a flu shot. Because Dan's coworkers, including Fred, now won't catch the flu from Dan, they benefit from the decision even though they had nothing to do with the transaction between Dan and the clinic where he paid for and received his shot. In other words, a market transaction—the sale of flu vaccine in the form of an injection—has generated a positive externality. A situation that creates a positive externality confers a benefit on a third party who is not involved in a transaction. How is this a market failure? It's a market failure

PUBLIC GOODS AS MARKET FAILURE

A particular type of market failure has to do with what is called a **public good**. The key characteristic of a public good is that it can't easily be divided, and so people can't easily be prevented from enjoying its benefits.

Most goods on the market are private goods—they can be divided, and people can be prevented from enjoying their benefits. But how, for example, can the owner of a lighthouse divide the illumination it produces? How can the lighthouse's owner sell pieces of that light to individual users?

As it happens, many lighthouses are privately owned, and lighthouse services are bundled into docking fees. But lighthouses have benefits that go beyond keeping large ships and smaller craft from crashing into harbors. If someone wants to enjoy the benefits of a lighthouse but doesn't want to pay the owner for the light, what can the owner do? After all, if the owner turns the light off so nonpayers can't use it, then paying customers will also be prevented from enjoying the lighthouse's benefits.

You can see what's likely to happen in the long run: The owner keeps the light burning, and more users simply decide not to pay for the light. (In economic parlance, these people are referred to as **free riders**.) Why would a profit-seeking entrepreneur choose to build a lighthouse when there are so many free riders who won't pay for the light? In a situation like this one, the government will have to step in and either provide the good outright or subsidize it.

Some have argued that sports stadiums are public goods that generate positive externalities, so they should receive public financing from local governments to build new stadiums. Even though some teams have been successful in convincing policymakers that sports stadiums are public goods, a stadium doesn't meet the economic definition of a public good. A stadium can easily be divided into boxes and seats. And it's easy to keep people from having access to the game inside the stadium. Customers must purchase tickets to enter the venue; anyone who shows up at the gate without one won't make it past the turnstiles.

in part because, thanks to Dan's decision to get a flu shot, Fred and all of Dan's other coworkers already have some level of protection from the flu, so they may decide not to get a flu shot themselves. Or maybe Fred and Dan's other coworkers make less money than Dan, or have other reasons to not pay for a flu shot. As a result, the manufacturer of the flu vaccine, knowing that the number of people who benefit from the vaccine tends to be disproportionately higher than the number of people who actually get a flu shot, will produce less of the vaccine than would be the case if everyone chose to get a flu shot, and private clinics or other for-profit facilities that offer flu shots will not be able to immunize as many people as they could. In other words—specifically, the words that an economist would use— the socially optimal level of production (output) is actually higher than the market outcome; the market doesn't produce enough of the good because it doesn't capture all the external benefits generated by the good's production.

The Need for Regulation

As we've just seen, market failure, by definition, involves a misallocation of resources. That is, when potential buyers don't have all the information they need, when a market is monopolized or insufficiently competitive, or when the sellers of a good don't pay the true costs or cannot capture all the benefits of the good's production, some kind of distortion has entered the relationship between buyers and sellers, and something has disturbed the market's equilibrium. These are situations in which some type of intervention on the part of the government may be warranted, and an alphabet soup of federal agencies has cropped up over the decades to deal with market failures like the ones just described.

Because markets work better when truthful and accurate information is available to consumers, the Federal Trade Commission (FTC), among its other duties, regulates advertising in the United States and can come down hard on a company if its advertising practices are found to be deceptive. The Food and Drug Administration (FDA) imposes labeling requirements on manufacturers of food products and medications. The Securities and Exchange Commission (SEC) requires that publicly traded companies regularly disclose certain kinds of information to the public.

When market failure arises from lack of competition, the FTC and the Department of Justice (DOJ) share the duty of cracking down on anticompetitive practices. At times, even the Federal Bureau of Investigation (FBI) gets involved in this arena (for example, by investigating suspected collusion among firms).

When it comes to negative externalities involving pollution, the primary regulatory agency is the Environmental Protection Agency (EPA), which attempts to limit or eliminate various types of pollution by levying taxes, imposing fines and restrictions, and applying other regulatory measures. For example, some EPA regulations can force a manufacturing firm to "scrub" its emissions by requiring the firm to invest in special equipment. Whatever form the environmental regulation takes, its result will be to limit not only the polluting firm's harm to the environment but also the total production, or output, of the good that the firm manufactures. In this way, regulation moves the output in this market toward the socially optimal level.

Positive externalities, if recognized by the government, are typically dealt with through some form of *subsidy*, or financial support in the form of a cash payment or tax reduction. For example, if a particular type of immunization created substantial external benefits, then the government might choose to subsidize private clinics that offer the immunization, thus allowing the clinics to immunize more people. Another approach might be to offer subsidies to individual consumers so they can more easily afford to be immunized. A third approach

The Federal Trade Commission was established in 1914 by President Wilson as part of antitrust efforts aimed at protecting consumers and competitiveness.

might be to set up government-funded clinics and let the government provide the immunizations. A fourth possibility might be for the government simply to require that citizens are immunized. Whichever approach is used, there would be a rise in both total vaccine production and immunization, and the output in this market would move toward the socially optimal level.

Market Failure versus Failure of Market Outcomes

In 1999, a man attempted to auction off one of his kidneys on eBay. Bidding on the organ climbed to over $5.75 million before the company noticed and shut the auction down. (It's a felony to sell body parts in the United States, and eBay doesn't allow illegal goods to be sold on its site.)

Some people were surprised, perhaps even shocked, by this incident. How could someone even think of selling a part of his body online, and who were the people bidding on it?

Here we have an example of a market outcome that was widely unpopular and even caused revulsion in some people. But this was not a case of market failure. In fact, the market did exactly what a market is supposed to do.

- There was a supply: exactly one kidney. (Some might argue that the market was monopolized, since there was only one seller offering one kidney, but until the auction was shut down, nothing prevented anyone else from offering another kidney for sale.)

- There was clear demand, as indicated by the bids that pushed the price into the millions.

- There was apparently sound information about the kidney.

- There were no externalities.

Thus the market actually appeared to be working very well. It was the outcome of that market—its very existence, you might say—that people didn't like, and that created the problem.

There are plenty of other situations in which markets do what they're supposed to do even when people (or governments) don't approve of the outcomes. Markets exist for illegal drugs, weapons, prostitution, and many other goods and activities that people find unsavory and governments find problematic. There are even places in the world where babies are bought and sold.

Nothing reveals human tastes as well as markets do; you can ask people what they like, but you won't get nearly as honest an answer as when you observe what they're actually buying. None of the commerce just described is due to market failure. Those markets exist because there are people willing to sell certain goods and other people willing to pay money for them. Markets are completely nonjudgmental. They have no morality built

THE MARKET FOR MARIJUANA

The discussion about the regulation of marijuana is complex. To some extent, the market for marijuana falls into the category of markets with outcomes that violate social standards (or the social standards of some people). But a case can also be made that marijuana use creates negative externalities, much in the way that polluting activities do. For example, some people may choose to drive while stoned, and someone who has grown psychologically dependent on marijuana may lose all motivation to work and then become dependent on public aid, too.

Advocates for legalizing marijuana argue that alcohol also generates precisely these kinds of social costs, and to a much greater extent than marijuana does. After all, the marijuana advocates say, alcohol impairs judgment and lowers inhibitions, making someone more likely to engage in illegal activities, and yet alcohol is perfectly legal.

Another argument for legalization is that cannabis has medicinal effects and, as such, creates substantial benefits for society.

Then there's the argument that so many libertarian-leaning people have been making for years: People are going to use marijuana anyway, so why not legalize it, regulate it, and tax it? Underlying this argument is the idea that a market for marijuana exists, has existed for a long time, and is not going away any time soon.

Everyone who knows even a little about history knows that alcohol prohibition in the United States in the 1920s and early 1930s didn't really work. There were places people could go to find alcohol "under the table," so to speak. Prohibition was enacted partly for moral reasons but also because of the negative externalities that alcohol consumption caused. Women who belonged to the temperance groups that played such a big part in pushing prohibition were fed up with the behavior of their husbands and other male family members when under the influence of alcohol.

From an economic standpoint, it's difficult to argue that alcohol should be legal and marijuana should not. In fact, the economics of the two markets are very similar, or at least they would be if marijuana, now approved for use in a few states, were legal to the extent that alcohol currently is. No doubt social attitudes have played a bigger role than economics in keeping laws against marijuana on the books.

Clearly, though, attitudes are rapidly shifting. It's easy to imagine the day, not too many years in the future, when the sale of marijuana is legal in every state in the union. But the market for legal marijuana, like the market for alcohol, will almost certainly be more tightly regulated than the markets for most other goods.

into them. That's one reason why a government may decide to regulate a market: the market's activity doesn't conform to acceptable social standards.

A case in point is the market in prostitution. In the Old West, the prostitution market worked the way a market is supposed to work, and could not be regulated on the basis of arguments about the market's failure. But when prostitution eventually came to be seen as an unsavory activity, laws against it were established even though the prostitution market had always worked very well. The arguments for the prostitution market's regulation had more to do with ethics and morality than with economics.

Regulation based on morality may be entirely justified, particularly in certain egregious circumstances, such as the buying and selling of babies. An important thing to keep in mind, however, is that social standards and notions of morality and ethics can change over time.

PRICE CONTROLS AS AN EXAMPLE OF GOVERNMENT REGULATION

Government intervention in markets can take several forms. Limits on emissions, zoning restrictions, gun ownership laws, labeling restrictions—these are examples of the tens of thousands of regulations that exist in the United States. There aren't enough pages in this book to cover in detail all the different forms that government intervention takes, so let's focus now on one particular form of intervention: price controls.

Aside from government restrictions on a company's or industry's level of output, price controls are the most direct form of government intervention in a market, and they potentially have the greatest impact. Price controls are limits on market prices. A **price ceiling** is a maximum price allowed by law, and a **price floor** is a minimum price required by law.

Price Ceilings

When a price ceiling has been established, sellers are not allowed to charge more for a particular good than the price set by the government. The problem with price ceilings is that they change the incentives in a market.

Gasoline Price Controls

Suppose the price of gasoline is $2.50 per gallon, and that there are one million gallons of gas bought and sold every day. Now suppose that the government, judging $2.50 per gallon as too high a price for gas, decides to help people out by setting a price ceiling to $1.50 per gallon.

Will the price ceiling really help people out? Let's see what happens.

As we know, consumers wanted and were able to buy one million gallons of gasoline every day before the price ceiling was lowered to $1.50 per gallon. But now, given the new, artificially low price, they want two million gallons per day. But why would sellers want to put two million gallons per day on the market? At the lower price, they won't even be willing to offer one million gallons per day. Some sellers already don't operate efficiently enough, so if the price ceiling is set at $1.50 per gallon, those sellers will be forced to shut down. Sellers who do manage to remain in business may be willing to offer only 250,000 gallons per day at the price of $1.50, and so a shortage of 1.75 million gallons of gasoline will develop in the gasoline market.

Even if we ignore the additional demand spurred by the artificially lower price of $1.50 per gallon, there will still be 750,000 fewer gallons available every day than there were before the lower price ceiling was put into effect. Imagine the long lines at the gas stations, the stations running out of fuel or rationing gasoline, and all the angry customers arriving at the pumps after spending hours in line, only to discover that the gas supply has run out.

Rent Controls

In the first decade of the 21st century, a new political party appeared on the scene, mainly in New York City. The Rent Is Too Damn High Party, by virtue of its name, simultaneously announced its primary issue and its position on that issue. The party has nominated candidates for various state and local offices, and even though the party's candidates have never come close to winning an election, plenty of politicians agree with the party's platform.

Rent controls have been enacted in New York City and other US cities. These are another form of price ceiling. Most rent control systems limit the frequency of allowable rent increases as well as the amount of any increases. In some

cities, rent controls only apply to larger rental unit complexes in the regulated area.

Rent controls are certainly a well-intentioned regulation, but most mainstream economists see them as leading to problems. For one thing, rent controls produce shortages of rental units in the regulated areas. For another, they have the effect of reducing the quality of the available rental units—if landlords are not able to charge market rates, then their profits are squeezed, and they're less willing to spend money on repairs and updates. In addition, prospective landlords are less likely to build new rental units in areas that have rent controls. The takeaway is that a regulation intended to help people acquire and retain affordable housing has had the net effect of reducing the supply as well as the quality of affordable housing.

Price Floors

When a price floor is in effect, the government requires sellers to charge buyers a specified minimum amount for a good or service. Like a price ceiling, a price floor changes incentives in ways that distort the market. As experience shows, a price floor may come with other unintended consequences.

The Minimum Wage

Where the federal minimum wage is concerned, the relevant market is the market for low-skilled or unskilled labor. Here, the sellers are the workers, and the buyers are the employers. When this price floor is in effect, the government doesn't allow sellers (workers)

Bronx tenements, pictured here in 1936, are one example of a rent control scheme that had the unintended consequence of giving landlords no incentive to maintain high-quality units.

to charge buyers (employers) less than a certain amount of money per hour.

It may seem confusing for the minimum wage to be defined in this way. Maybe you're not accustomed to thinking of the minimum wage as an amount that the worker is required to charge the employer, but that's exactly the way economists talk about the minimum wage. If you wanted experience in a particular industry and were willing to work for less than the minimum wage, you would undoubtedly find someone to pay you at a lower rate, but it would actually be illegal for you to sell your labor for less than the minimum wage.

The minimum wage was established to alleviate and prevent certain abuses in the workplace, and it has a long and involved history. It may seem like a compassionate measure, but it leads to at least one serious unintended consequence—some amount of unemployment (and, many economists would add, increases in some prices, and therefore higher inflation).

If you don't believe that, imagine what would happen if the government were to set a federal minimum wage of, say, $50 per hour. There would be a lot of layoffs, with some firms getting by with a skeleton crew and others forced to close their doors for good. Huge numbers of workers would also be replaced by various kinds of labor-saving technology. The minimum wage doesn't even have to be as high as $50 per hour before these effects kick in. They're already occurring, to some extent, at the actual minimum wage.

Like rent controls, the minimum wage developed from good intentions. Like every other kind of regulation, the minimum wage has benefits and costs that should be carefully considered, regardless of policymakers' good intentions.

The Living Wage

One big criticism of the federal minimum wage is that it doesn't account for geographic differences in the cost of living. The living wage is intended to correct that shortcoming.

The movement for a living wage gained prominence in the United States in the 1990s. The idea behind this policy is that the minimum wage doesn't provide enough income for a family, or even an individual, to live on without some type of support from the government. Therefore, although the precise definition of what constitutes a living wage is somewhat different from place to place, the living wage is set at a level higher than the minimum wage so that workers can pay the typical costs of food, shelter, clothing, healthcare, and other basic needs in the regions where they live.

The living wage, like the minimum wage, has led to higher unemployment in the cities and regions where it has been implemented. Like the minimum wage, the living wage also tends to raise prices and increase the likelihood of inflation. In addition, as firms relocate to areas where this price floor is not in effect, economic decline occurs in those regions where policymakers have mandated a wage higher than the federally mandated minimum wage.

ETHANOL: A FARM-TO-FORK CAUTIONARY TALE

At one time, most of the corn grown in the United States went to feed people and livestock. Now, much less of the US corn crop is used that way, and livestock get more than humans do. What happened? Large amounts of corn are now being used as biofuel for automobiles, in the form of ethanol.

Environmental concerns were the primary reason for biofuel mandates in the United States and elsewhere. When the mandates were established, biofuels were thought to be cleaner than petroleum-based fuels, and therefore better for the environment. Policymakers also believed that a shift to biofuels would lower the US dependence on foreign oil.

But there may be no net benefit associated with switching from fossil fuels to biofuels when it comes to carbon dioxide emissions and their connection to climate change. Not only that, but the production of biofuels has environmental consequences of its own, such as land and water depletion, and policymakers apparently didn't take these factors into account when they established the mandates. Nor is it clear that the use of biofuels has reduced US reliance on foreign oil—when ethanol is blended with gasoline, it essentially waters the gas down and reduces the amount of energy it can provide, which means that consumers burning ethanol have to use more gas to drive the same distances they covered when they were burning gasoline alone.

These are all serious consequences of the biofuel mandates, but the biggest consequence has been the impact on the corn market itself. Farmland that once fed people and livestock is now being used to support transportation needs. The subsidies paid to farmers growing corn for ethanol have pushed up the price of US corn. And because the United States is such a large producer, that price increase has affected the world market, too, and is especially burdensome for consumers in less developed countries. Imagine the effect on children's nutrition in a country where corn tortillas are a food staple.

No one would claim that the purpose of biofuel mandates in the United States was to starve children in Central America, but the whole situation clearly shows the law of unintended consequences in action. It's also an example of government failure on a global scale.

Agricultural Price Supports

Agricultural price supports are a special case of government-imposed price controls. In many countries, including the United States, the government engages in some form of price support for farmers. The goal of such support is to stabilize the incomes of farmers (low-income farmers in particular).

A price support for agriculture could take the form of a price floor—a minimum price that must be paid for agricultural products (output)—but that's not the most typical way that an agricultural price support works. In the United States, agricultural price supports have been carried out in a variety of other ways.

One way involves the government purchasing farmers' output at some predetermined target price. When the government does this, the purchased supply must be handled in some manner that won't reduce demand or dilute the price in the particular market. In some agricultural markets (grains, for example), the government has sought to stabilize prices by purchasing excess supplies, storing that surplus, and releasing it for sale later on when production is down.

In another arrangement, the government pays farmers to set some land aside and not use it to grow certain crops. With supplies of these crops artificially reduced, their market prices rise. In this scheme, the government is, in effect, paying farmers not to produce—the exact opposite of how most subsidies work.

Some analysts argue that without government intervention, farmers' incomes would be unduly volatile—in lean years, many small farmers could be forced out of business, with unknown effects for the country's future food security. Other analysts point out that farmers have other ways to stabilize their incomes, such as purchasing crop insurance or entering into contracts to sell their future crops at particular fixed prices (a farmer who does this is said to be buying agricultural futures as a hedge against bad outcomes).

The jury is still out on how effective agricultural price supports really are. They do help farmers, but there is also evidence suggesting that most of the support goes to large producers rather than low-income farm families. These price supports also push up the price of agricultural land, so young farmers find it more difficult to get started and to expand their operations. There's no question that agricultural price supports have also led to the creation of large government bureaucracies, which themselves require operating resources. Remember what we said on page 33 about opportunity costs? Resources devoted to running government agencies are not available for improving schools, building roads, conducting medical research, and carrying out other important public and civic endeavors.

GOVERNMENT FAILURE

If a market failure occurs, the government's intervention may be justified. But it's also true that the government doesn't always offer the best solution. Politicians and bureaucrats may end up making things worse or even creating a whole new problem—a situation known as **government failure**. Sometimes the best solution comes from the market itself.

Government failure can occur for a number of reasons:

- Although the government tracks and monitors vast amounts of information, sometimes even the government doesn't have the information it needs to solve a particular problem. Bad information can often lead to a bad solution.

- Even when good, reliable information is available, red tape can lead to a slow or inadequate response that ends up compounding the problem.

- A market failure may involve multiple complex systems, and a change to one part of a system can lead to unforeseen effects in another part of that system or even in a different system. (Remember the law of unintended consequences we discussed on page 30?)

- Without impugning the character of elected representatives in general, we can observe that government failure

sometimes occurs because particular politicians may be more focused on getting re-elected, making deals with one another, or achieving some purpose other than implementing policy measures that are truly in the best interests of their constituents.

Given the risk for government failure, wouldn't it be better for the government to stay out of markets altogether? In some cases, it would indeed be better for the government to sit on the sidelines and let the market run free, even in the presence of some type of market failure. In other cases, government intervention makes the market better and promotes society's well-being.

There's no one-size-fits-all approach to determining when there's an economic basis for government intervention in a failed market, so it's wise for officials to examine the costs and benefits of sitting the failure out, versus intervening to solve the problem. If the benefits of the government's intervention will be outweighed by the costs, then the government should stay out of the market. Conversely, if the benefits of intervention will be greater than the costs, then an economic basis for government regulation exists. Of course, estimating the costs and benefits of proposed regulation is a complicated, time-consuming, and potentially controversial task—exactly the kind of task that will keep economists employed in this country for a long time to come.

FREE MARKETS & REGULATIONS

1874

General Equilibrium Theory

Léon Walras develops a mathematical model that demonstrates how supply and demand lead to general equilibrium and how free markets could be naturally stable.

1900

Lacey Act

Designed to protect parts of the environment, Congress passes the Lacey Act prohibiting the sale or purchase of wildlife or plant life that is illegally obtained.

1920

Prohibition

Under the 18th amendment, the US government outlaws the consumption or sale of any alcoholic beverages. Prohibition lasts for 13 years in the United States.

1890

Supply and Demand

Building on the work of Classical economics, British economist Alfred Marshall contends that the value of a product is determined by supply and demand principles.

1906

Food and Drug Regulation

Congress passes the Pure Food and Drug Act that prohibits interstate commerce of mislabeled and adulterated food and drugs. It eventually leads to the creation of the Food and Drug Administration (FDA).

1943

Rent Regulation

The federal government administers New York's rent control program, which limits the amount a landlord can charge a tenant for rent. The state takes over management in 1950. It is the longest-running rent stabilization program in the US.

1981

Minimum Wage

President Reagan's administration is the only one to not raise the minimum wage. During his eight-year term, the minimum wage remained at $3.35 per hour while prices rose.

2012

Legalizing Marijuana

Voters in Colorado and Washington state approve initiatives to legalize the recreational use and sale of marijuana for adults age 21 and over. Alaska and Oregon enact similar laws in 2015.

1944

Spontaneous Order

In his book, *The Road to Serfdom*, Friedrich Hayek argues that market economies produce efficient and spontaneous order, and any attempts from government to impose collective order would fail.

1994

Living Wage

Labor and religious leaders in Baltimore are successful in their fight for a living wage for city workers. Community advocates win similar ordinances in other cities including San Francisco, Los Angeles, and Boston.

FOR
SALE

4 COMPETITION, MONOPOLIES, & ANTITRUST LAWS

Not all industries and markets are created the same. Some are highly competitive, featuring vibrant interaction among large numbers of sellers and buyers, while other markets are dominated by a small handful of companies. Some markets have been completely monopolized—sometimes with the full knowledge and permission of government regulators. In a partly or completely monopolized market, buyers have no choice but to purchase a good or service from a small number of sellers or a single seller. To promote competition between firms and to limit or prevent monopolies, governments enact and enforce antitrust laws. This chapter explores the concepts and issues relating to competition, monopoly, and antitrust. We'll examine the factors that make an industry more competitive versus less competitive. We'll also look at what happens when a single firm amasses too much power in a market, as well as the history and workings of antitrust legislation in the United States.

COMPETITIVE VERSUS NONCOMPETITIVE MARKETS

A market or industry characterized by **perfect competition** has so many sellers of a good or a service that no individual seller can influence the market price; each one is just another drop in the proverbial bucket. This kind of market or industry is so easy for a new seller to enter that virtually any budding entrepreneur can go into business and compete with other sellers.

The products in a perfectly competitive market, and even in a market that is highly if not perfectly competitive, tend to be standardized (e.g., commodities like gold, agricultural products, and foreign currency). Firms in perfectly competitive markets may earn large profits in the short run (e.g., after the introduction of a new product). Over a longer period, however, competition tends to drive prices down, and profits tend to stabilize at a particular level.

The opposite of a perfectly competitive market is a market that's monopolized. As most people know, thanks to a famous board game featuring fake money and "get out of jail free" cards, a firm has a monopoly when it controls a market. The product or service that a monopoly firm sells has no close substitutes. People who want that good or service have to buy it from the monopolist.

If a firm is the only seller of a particular good or service, the firm is said to have a **pure monopoly** on that good or service. Sometimes a firm is also considered to have a monopoly if it dominates a small number of competitors in its market. For example, Microsoft isn't the world's only producer of computer operating systems, but Microsoft is so dominant in its market that the company has been accused of wielding monopoly power.

A market can also be an oligopoly, one that consists of a few large firms or is dominated by a few large firms. Auto manufacturing, aircraft manufacturing, the music industry, and the national mass media are good examples of oligopolistic industries. In an oligopoly, each firm's actions greatly affect its competitors.

(Opposite) Professional licensing hinders entry into a market, thereby limiting competition in fields ranging from hairstyling to law and opening the door to monopoly power.

MONOPOLIES

Monopolies arise when there are barriers to entry, or factors that prevent competitors from entering a firm's market. One barrier to entry is when it's most efficient for a single firm to supply an entire market (for example, it may make more sense to have one electric company in town than to have hundreds of competing companies with their own grids). In this situation, the firm is said to have a **natural monopoly**. Another type of barrier is a **resource monopoly**, with a single firm controlling all access to a necessary input. There are also legal barriers to entry, such as patents, trademarks, and copyrights.

The requirement for occupational licenses—for everyone from doctors and lawyers to hair stylists and taxi drivers—can also be viewed as a barrier to entry. Such licensure requirements may be intended to keep some potential competitors out of a market, and thus to protect the monopoly power of current license holders. To justify the requirements for many types of occupational licenses, policymakers cite concerns about public safety. This explanation makes sense when it comes to licensing emergency medical technicians and other allied health professionals. It's less convincing as an explanation for requiring residential painting contractors or installers of home entertainment systems to be licensed. And it's especially unconvincing when members of occupational associations, rather than consumers, are the ones demanding licensure.

In this situation, it's hard to avoid the conclusion that practitioners in those occupations seek to limit the number of their potential competitors.

Common Misconceptions about Monopolies

Even people who follow business trends may harbor misconceptions about monopolies. One misconception is that monopoly firms are guaranteed high profits. It's true, of course, that if a company has a market monopolized, the company stands to earn a much higher profit than it would if the market were competitive. But high profits are definitely not guaranteed. In fact, a monopolist isn't guaranteed any profit at all. Many people think of monopoly firms as large, powerful concerns with deep pockets, and some of them certainly fit that description. But it's also possible for a company to have a monopoly on a product or service for which there isn't enough demand to generate a profit. In a particular year, for example, patents may be granted for a few hundred thousand products, some of which will generate large profits for their owners, who are authorized as the products' exclusive sellers for a period of time. But what about a firm that holds a patent for a product that nobody wants? That kind of monopoly would be unprofitable indeed.

Another misconception is that a monopolist necessarily charges the very highest possible price for its product or service. But how could that be true? Just like any other firm, a monopoly firm has demand for its product or service. Consider a company that is a community's only provider of cable TV and Internet services. Maybe 1 percent of the people in the community would be willing to pay $1,000 per month for TV and Internet access, but the other 99 percent would balk at such an exorbitant rate. Because this monopoly firm wants to maximize its profit, it can't charge the highest price that a tiny minority of its customers would be willing to pay. If it did, it would lose the vast majority of the market. The firm's customers would simply find other alternatives.

One of the biggest misconceptions about monopolies is that they're always bad. Some people even think that monopoly firms and the executives who run them are evil. But the fact is that many monopolies create extraordinary value, not just for stockholders, managers, and employees, but for society as a whole. For example, most public utility companies enjoy monopoly status, and while a local gas or electric company may hear its share of justified complaints from customers, such utility companies nonetheless do an outstanding job of providing energy on a 24/7 basis. Besides, some products (certain lifesaving drugs, for example) might never have become available at all if their inventors and developers hadn't

While the natural monopoly over public utilities may seem unfair to some consumers, it is perhaps the best way to ensure efficient delivery of essential goods like electricity.

been granted patents and monopoly power for long enough to recoup the costs of research and development.

Identifying Monopolies

There are measures that economists can use to determine how competitive an industry is. The two principal measures are *concentration ratios* and the *Herfindahl-Hirschman Index (HHI)*.

When the "four-firm concentration ratio" of an industry is calculated, the result shows the market share of the four largest firms in an industry as a proportion of the industry's total sales. For example, suppose an industry is composed of six firms. One firm has 40 percent of the market, another firm has 30 percent of the market, two firms each have 10 percent of the market, and two more firms each have 5 percent of the market. Together, the four largest firms—the one with 40 percent of the market, the one with 30 percent, and the two with 10 percent each—have 90 percent of the market, and so the four-firm concentration ratio for this industry is 90. A ratio of 90 indicates high market concentration, or a market that is not very competitive (a ratio of 40 or higher usually implies that a market is oligopolistic).

Calculation of the HHI is somewhat more involved. The HHI's potential values may be as low as nearly zero (for a very highly competitive industry) and as high as 10,000 (for an industry whose market is limited to one

COLLUSION: A SPECIAL CASE OF MONOPOLY

In *The Wealth of Nations,* Adam Smith wrote that when sellers of the same product get together for any reason, buyers should watch out for their wallets. Smith was warning about a problem as old as commerce itself: **collusion,** sometimes known as *price fixing* or *bid rigging.*

We've seen that every firm in an oligopolistic market is extremely sensitive to the effects of the actions taken by the other firms in that market. For example, if one of the firms drastically cuts its prices, then the other firms, reeling from the impact, will respond with price cuts of their own. But none of the firms wants the race to the bottom that would ensue if they all continued competing on that basis, and this is why the incentive to collude is so strong. If they're able to act together, the firms can make production and pricing decisions that benefit all of them (at the expense of consumers, of course). In other words, the colluding firms can behave as if they were one big firm. They will become a de facto monopoly, and this arrangement allows them to extract substantially larger profits from consumers than they would otherwise be able to. A group of businesses engaged in collusion is commonly referred to as a **cartel**.

The Organization of the Petroleum Exporting Countries (OPEC) is probably the best-known cartel in the world. Its member countries don't have a 100 percent (pure) monopoly in crude oil production and the trade of petroleum, but they control a large enough share of the market to exert significant influence on world oil prices. In October 1973, what was then the Organization of Arab Petroleum Exporting Countries colluded to cut production and reduce exports to the United States and other countries. Lines of cars waiting to fill up at US gas stations stretched around whole blocks. Eventually gas was rationed, and the nation's truck drivers staged a two-day strike. Within six months, the price of crude oil had gone up 400 percent, and economic pain persisted around the world into the 1980s.

OPEC can act as a cartel because its members are sovereign nations, which means they're not subject to the laws of other nations and can even evade the laws that regulate private companies within the individual members' own borders. In the United States and many other countries, however, collusion is illegal, and conviction on a charge of collusion carries hefty fines and jail time.

Collusion still crops up frequently in the United States in a wide array of industries. Recent investigations by the US Department of Justice have targeted airlines, book publishers, investment firms, food manufacturers, distributors and retailers of compact discs, professional sports organizations, and manufacturers of agricultural additives, to name just a few cases.

Monopoly can easily create chaos, such as when the OPEC oil cartel's cut in production left American drivers in long lines at gasoline stations.

seller, a purely monopolistic scenario). The US Department of Justice, one of the agencies that has a hand in regulating monopolies, typically sees an HHI between 1,500 and 2,500 as indication of moderate market concentration, and an HHI higher than 2,500 as indication of high market concentration. If a proposed merger in a highly concentrated market seemed likely to increase the HHI by more than 200 points, then the merger might face government opposition on the grounds that it would unduly decrease competition if allowed to proceed.

Monopolistic Competitors

A firm that can be characterized as a monopolistic competitor has features of a monopoly firm as well as features of a firm that operates in a perfectly competitive market. The monopolistic competitor does enjoy a monopoly, but only when it comes to its own brand; in contrast to the pure monopolist, and there are close substitutes for the monopolistic competitor's product. Because of these close substitutes, the monopolistic competitor may earn profits higher than normal in the short run but will merely break even in the long run, just as a firm operating in a perfectly competitive market might. Retail stores, fast-food restaurants, clothing makers, and hair salons are examples of monopolistic competitors. In fact, most businesses are monopolistic competitors.

Monopolistic competitors tend to engage heavily in advertising, promotion, and product differentiation. A monopolistic competitor's goal is to convince consumers that there really are no close substitutes for its product, even though that's actually not the case. In other words, the monopolistic competitor tries to become more like a monopoly firm and less like a firm operating in a perfectly competitive market.

There are pros and cons associated with the monopolistic competitor's heavy emphasis on product differentiation and advertising. People like having choices, of course, and so some amount of product differentiation is good. But do consumers really need the dozens of varieties of shampoo and designer jeans and breakfast cereals and razor blades that monopolistic competitors offer? Or could the resources devoted to product differentiation and promotion be used in a way that brings more benefit to society?

ANTITRUST REGULATION AND ENFORCEMENT

In a market that's sufficiently competitive, the government doesn't need to do anything to ensure a socially optimal outcome unless there's a market failure. If the firms in a competitive market are enjoying substantial profits, then other enterprising sellers will enter that market, and the new competition can be expected to drive prices down for buyers while prompting sellers to innovate and to improve the quality of their products and services. This kind of adjustment can happen in a competitive market because a competitive market doesn't present high barriers to entry, so it's relatively inexpensive for new sellers to wade in. In a monopolized market, this kind of adjustment can't happen. As a result, the government has long sought both to regulate firms that have monopoly power and, at times, to restrict the formation of monopolies in the first place.

All regulation comes with costs, regardless of its good intentions, and antitrust regulation is no exception. In any type of government action, however, what ultimately matters is whether its benefits outweigh its costs. The economic justification for regulating a monopoly is that monopolistic practices tend to create higher prices and lower levels of output than would exist in a competitive market, and such outcomes aren't socially optimal. In the United States and many other countries, the costs associated with breaking up a monopoly, policing a company's business practices, blocking a merger, or pursuing other forms of antitrust enforcement come with the same intended benefit: promotion of competition and prevention of anticompetitive behavior.

At the federal level, responsibility for enforcing the nation's antitrust laws rests with the Federal Trade Commission (FTC) and the US Department of Justice. Sometimes other agencies also get involved. For example, the Federal Communications Commission (FCC) typically participates in antitrust cases involving telecommunications companies. At the state level, each state's attorney general, along with the relevant state agencies, is responsible for enforcing that state's antitrust laws.

Review of Mergers and Acquisitions

One of the primary ways for the government to limit the formation of monopolies is to review proposed mergers and not allow some of them to go through. The government can use concentration ratios and the HHI to calculate whether a merger will leave an industry's market with too little competition. In 2011, for example, AT&T announced its intention to acquire a competitor, T-Mobile, but the Department of Justice filed an antitrust lawsuit to block the proposed merger and the plan was dropped.

Merger cases can become very political. The standards for approving a merger are not static, and a new presidential administration can change them, as the Obama administration did when it revised a set of guidelines to make particular types of mergers more difficult. The fact that some administrations have allowed mergers that probably would have failed under other administrations implies that a certain amount of discretion exists in the enforcement of antitrust laws.

Price-Based Antitrust Regulation

Not all monopolies are created through mergers and acquisitions, and the government also must contend with monopolies that come about by other means. Like proposed mergers, cases like these can be affected by political bias and may entail some discretion in antitrust enforcement.

The government may choose to regulate a monopoly firm by imposing a price ceiling

ANTITRUST LEGISLATION IN THE UNITED STATES: A BRIEF HISTORY

In the 19th century, monopolies like Standard Oil and US Steel were referred to as *trusts*. At some point, the government came to perceive these big firms as a problem. In an effort to keep the trusts, or monopolies, in check, Congress went to work and began passing antitrust laws. The Sherman Act was passed in 1890 and was the first such law. It made price fixing and other forms of collusion illegal while also outlawing monopolization.

The Sherman Act turned out to be too vague, and in 1914 Congress passed the Clayton Act to clarify the Sherman Act's ambiguities. The Clayton Act was designed to prevent mergers that would allow owners of firms to create de facto monopolies.

The act also prohibited price discrimination of an anticompetitive nature, such as the practice of charging a price below the cost of production with the intent of driving competitors out of the market.

Also in 1914, the Federal Trade Commission Act established the Federal Trade Commission (FTC) and gave the FTC authority to investigate unfair business practices. The act was later amended, and the FTC gained the power to police the advertising practices of the nation's businesses as well.

Today the FTC works in conjunction with the US Department of Justice to enforce the nation's antitrust laws. Because all 50 states also have their own antitrust laws, which are enforced by each state's attorney general, such regulation of monopolizing activity nationwide may be saving US consumers millions and perhaps even billions of dollars each year.

This 1904 cartoon shows a Standard Oil "octopus" with its tentacles around the steel and copper industries, along with a few branches of government.

INNOVATION VERSUS MONOPOLY

Some economists—such as Milton Friedman—have theorized that in an occupational market without licensure requirements, incompetent practitioners would be weeded out, and those who earned the best reputations would be rewarded. Friedman died in 2006, three years too soon to witness the launch of Uber, the unregulated rideshare company that uses a proprietary smartphone app to compete on its own terms with regulated taxi services. It's probably a safe bet that Friedman would have endorsed Uber's business model.

It's too early to say whether Uber has proved Friedman's theory—Uber, a private company, is not required to disclose its revenues, and its expansion has not been without controversy. But it's not too early to say that Uber's model works, as demonstrated not only by the emergence of competitors like Lyft but also by the entry of companies like Airbnb, an unregulated competitor of highly regulated hotels and motels, into the so-called sharing economy.

As Uber shows, it's not always necessary for the government to intervene in monopolized or highly concentrated markets. Sometimes actors in the economy, using new technologies and innovative business models, challenge established monopolies and pave the way for competition.

The newspaper industry offers another excellent example of innovation trumping monopoly. For decades in the United States, it was common for a small or midsize city to be served by only one newspaper. In those one-paper towns, all local news was filtered through the editors of a single news department. Now, the advent of the Internet has widened the availability of news, both national and local, and brought it to readers at a much lower cost, with the added advantage of saving a few trees. What's been happening in the newspaper industry recalls what the economist Joseph Schumpeter called *creative destruction*. Sometimes competition and innovation degrade or even destroy entire industries while enabling the creation of others, and the Internet is one of these creatively destructive forces. It has created dozens of new industries while revolutionizing thousands of others, and it has destroyed or is on the way to destroying some industries as well. For example, many people—especially Millennials—now read everything online. By the time the Millennials are in their retirement years there probably won't be any print newspapers at all, thanks to online news. That's creative destruction in action.

In the best of circumstances, competition brings out the best in producers, rewards consumers with better products and better service at lower prices, promotes the efficient use of scarce resources, and, ultimately, makes all of society better off.

with the aim of achieving a market price close or equal to the price that would prevail in a competitive market. In the past, for example, some state agencies have set price caps on services offered by large local telephone companies. In a highly concentrated market, however, it's hard to get a price ceiling right because they must gauge what the competitive price would be in a market that has never been truly competitive.

Changes in telephone technology have also brought changes in the regulation of the telephone industry. Nowadays some local telephone companies, as well as many other utility companies, are regulated on the basis of their "rate of return," which means that the government sets prices for these firms' services in a way that restricts the firms to a predetermined level of profit. This type of regulation requires periodic examination to ensure that the specified rate of return is actually being achieved and that the monopoly firms aren't overearning.

Government regulators may also prevent a dominant firm from engaging in certain kinds of anticompetitive behavior such as **predatory pricing**, or the practice of setting a very low price, often below the cost of producing a good, so as to harm a competitor. Firms have also been fined for price fixing, a form of collusion that is a felony and is typically investigated by the Federal Bureau of Investigation (FBI), leading to prison time for some offenders.

Breakup of Monopolies

It takes a lot of time and money to break up a monopoly firm, so this is a step that the government doesn't take lightly. The government has sometimes taken action against monopolies it considered illegal, the most famous cases being the breakup of Standard Oil in 1911 and of AT&T in 1984.

In the first decade of the 21st century, Microsoft was nearly broken up into two separate companies after the government charged that it was illegally requiring computer manufacturers to preinstall its web browser, and penalizing manufacturers for promoting non-Microsoft products. In the end, the software giant avoided being broken up, but it was prevented from engaging in anticompetitive behavior by being ordered to pay billions of dollars to various parties harmed by its anticompetitive practices.

1908

The Edison Trust

A group of filmmakers centered mostly in New York form a trust between one another, essentially monopolizing the film industry by setting up restrictions and enforcements against would-be independent filmmakers.

1890

Sherman Antitrust Law

US Congress passes the landmark antitrust law in an effort to foil back-door monopolization deals between stockholders.

1914

Federal Trade Commission

The Federal Trade Commission is created to act as an independent agency to protect consumers from potentially unfair practices such as mergers between large companies.

1890

American Tobacco Company

The American Tobacco Company, formed by the Duke brothers, acquires over 150 tobacco factories, therefore monopolizing the vast majority of the American cigarette industry.

1914

Clayton Antitrust Act

The Clayton Act is passed as an amendment to the Sherman Antitrust law, by exempting unions from the antitrust legislation since workers needed the right to unionize in order to maintain bargaining power with employers.

1934

Communications Act

Signed into law by President Roosevelt, the act replaces the Federal Radio Commission with the Federal Communications Commission (FCC) for the purpose of regulating radio, television, and other means of communication in the United States.

1982

AT&T Breakup

The Department of Justice settles an antitrust case with AT&T in order to make room for "baby bells," or smaller telephone companies, to compete with the communications giant.

2013

Uber Settlement

The mobile cab company Uber is initially fined by the California Public Utilities Commission for operating cabs without a permit. However, Uber reaches a temporary settlement with the commission and continues growing.

1960

OPEC

An international oil cartel formed by several nations including Iran and Venezuela, the Organization of Petroleum Exporting Countries (OPEC), is designed to control the price and supply of oil across the globe.

2001

US vs. Microsoft Corporation

The Department of Justice alleges that Microsoft uses the efficiency and popularity of its Windows systems to prevent competitors from gaining market share. Microsoft loses the original case, but later reaches a settlement with the DOJ.

5 GLOBALIZATION & THE US ECONOMY

To some Americans, *globalization* is a bad word. People who are strongly critical of globalization see it as tantamount to shipping American factories and jobs abroad. It's true that some jobs in some industries have moved to other countries. But what opponents of globalization don't see, or perhaps choose not to acknowledge, is that globalization has brought tremendous benefits to the United States, just as it has to every other nation that has exchanged goods, services, people, and ideas with other nations. In this chapter, we'll examine the economics related to globalization and free international trade and look at the facts concerning US jobs lost to foreign nations. We'll also examine protectionism, which is essentially the opposite of free trade. In addition, we'll touch on the hot-button issue of immigration, which certainly belongs to the broader debate about globalization.

WHAT IS GLOBALIZATION, AND WHAT IS GOOD ABOUT IT?

Globalization is the process by which markets become integrated among nations. Aspects of globalization include international trade, foreign investment, and labor migration. Globalization entails more than just business activity; as the economies of different countries become increasingly integrated, there's also significant cultural exchange. Globalization permits the flow of goods, capital, labor, ideas, and culture across international borders. That flow may be regulated, but not entirely blocked.

Probably the most fundamental component of globalization is international trade, which entails the exchange of goods and services across international borders. International trade has been going on since before the establishment of the Silk Road, the ancient trade route that ran from China to the Mediterranean Sea. International trade must have involved some heavy costs in ancient times, since it required the use of overseas vessels or overland caravans, and so it must have offered some big advantages, too.

One reason why people engaged in international trade in centuries past was that they wanted goods that weren't available in their homelands. For example, if the Greeks wanted ivory, they would have had to import it, since Greece didn't produce ivory. That is still a reason why international trade persists, but it's not the primary reason. After all, even though some goods are found only in a few places, many others, especially manufactured goods, can be produced anywhere. The primary reason why countries continue to exchange goods and services is that they stand to gain a lot from specialization and trade.

Perhaps the easiest way to understand this principle is to forget about countries for a moment and just think about yourself. Imagine living all alone in a world with no specialization whatsoever. If there's anything you want or need in this no-specialization world, you have to make it yourself. You wake up in the morning and put on clothes that you sewed yourself, using fabric that you wove yourself, made of wool from the sheep you raised yourself, and the process goes on and on from there.

But, fortunately, that's not the kind of world we live in. We live in a world that features lots of specialization and trade on many levels.

Individuals don't try to produce everything themselves. Instead, most people specialize in some productive activity—accounting, construction, farming, game show hosting—and then use some of the fruits of their labor to buy goods and services from others who specialize in different kinds of productive activity. The same principle applies to companies, regions, nations, and even trading blocs.

When the production process is globalized, one country supplies the raw wool, while workers in another turn that wool into clothes to be shipped elsewhere.

Globalization and the Concept of Advantage

As individuals and as a nation, we don't try to produce every good at home. This is a point that Adam Smith himself addressed in *The Wealth of Nations*, where he introduced the concept of free trade based on absolute advantage. In his famous tome, he wrote, "It is the maxim of every prudent master of a family never to attempt to make at home what it will cost him more to make than to buy. The taylor [sic] does not attempt to make his own shoes, but buys them of the shoemaker. The

shoemaker does not attempt to make his own clothes, but employs a taylor [sic] ... If a foreign country can supply us with a commodity cheaper than we can make it, better buy it of them with some part of the produce of our own industry, employed in a way in which we have some advantage."

Absolute Advantage

In economics, a country is said to have an **absolute advantage** in producing a particular good if it can do so at a lower absolute cost, or per-unit cost, than a trading partner can. For example, the nations of Central America have an absolute advantage over Canada in banana production. Canada simply doesn't have the climate necessary for banana production. If you're good at fixing cars and your friend knows very little about how to do that, you have an absolute advantage over your friend in car repair, and you can fix your friend's car in exchange for your friend's help with your garden. These are examples of trade based on absolute advantage.

Comparative Advantage

Absolute advantage isn't the only basis on which trade occurs. David Ricardo, a British economist who lived in the late 18th and early 19th centuries, introduced the principle of **comparative advantage**. A country has a comparative advantage in producing a particular good when that country can produce the good at a lower opportunity cost than a trading partner can. In the context of trade, a nation's opportunity cost for producing a particular quantity of a good would consist of what the nation must give up to produce that good at that quantity. Remember, a nation's resources are scarce. If the nation directs its resources toward producing wicker brooms, then it won't have the resources to produce, say, wooden stools.

Consider a young woman, Hannah, who is very talented at website design and decides to start her own one-woman website design company. Designing websites is a big part of how Hannah will spend her time, of course, but she'll have to devote time to other tasks as well. In addition to designing websites, she's going to have to handle the marketing, bookkeeping, and administrative work. Hannah earns $45 per hour for her design work, but she earns nothing directly for all the behind-the-scenes work. As business picks up, she decides that it's time to hire an assistant to handle the administrative duties. She hires Robert, who is the best of the pool of applicants willing to work for the rate of pay Hannah is offering, say $15 per hour. Robert is a reliable worker, but he's not nearly as fast and efficient at administrative work as Hannah is—it takes him three hours to do work that she can get done in two hours. But Hannah still benefits greatly from Robert's efforts. At this stage of her company's development, it's better for the entrepreneur to spend more of her time on website design and less of her time on paperwork. For every additional hour that Hannah can work on website design at an hourly rate of $45, she will be able to pay Robert for three hours of work. In other words, she has an absolute advantage over Robert in both website design and administrative work because in both areas she's better and faster

David Ricardo (1772–1823) was a wealthy English stockbroker and economic theorist whose concept of comparative advantage among nations has served as a central tenet of globalization.

than him. But Hannah's opportunity cost of doing administrative work is too high, in view of the income she loses by not using all her time to work on website design. Therefore, Robert has a comparative advantage over Hannah in administrative work.

A particular country may not have an absolute advantage in producing any one good, but every country has a comparative advantage over potential trading partners in producing some good. If each of two countries has a comparative advantage in producing a particular good, and if each of those countries trades that good with the other country, then both countries benefit by becoming more prosperous. The rest of the world benefits, too, because the planet's scarce resources are used more efficiently. It's even possible to argue that international trade promotes world peace. Wouldn't a country think twice before declaring war on its best customer or best supplier? Thanks to international trade we have access to goods from all over the world. In addition, competition from foreign producers keeps our domestic producers on their toes. Domestic firms must strive to produce high-quality products in an efficient manner, and offer those products at prices consumers are willing to pay. Without international trade many of the goods we purchase on a regular basis would be more expensive. Free international trade has proven so beneficial that the majority of nations in the world have entered into free trade agreements with other nations.

Globalization and Multinational Corporations

Another important aspect of globalization has been the spread of the **multinational corporation**, which is a firm that operates and owns assets in more than one country. The typical multinational corporation has a central office in a home country. There are several reasons why a corporation might decide to become a multinational firm.

- By locating a branch or subsidiary in another country, it's easier for the corporation to tap into that country's demand for its product.

- The corporation may be able to save on transportation costs by shipping goods from its foreign subsidiary.

- Labor costs may be lower in the country where the firm has located its foreign subsidiary.

- Where regulations, taxes, and potential subsidies are concerned, the corporation that has a branch or subsidiary in another country may be able to receive "national treatment" from that country, which means it will be treated the same as the country's domestic firms.

It can be advantageous for a corporation to become a multinational firm by establishing branches or subsidiaries in other countries instead of simply exporting goods to those countries.

Globalization and Currency Valuations

The **foreign exchange market** is where the currencies of the various nations are traded. Yet unlike, say, the New York Stock Exchange, this particular market doesn't have a central location, and it doesn't close at night or on the weekends and holidays. The foreign exchange market is also where each currency's **exchange rate**—its price relative to other nations' currencies—is determined.

There was a time when most of the world's currencies were pegged to gold. Later, for a period of time after World War II, the United States pegged the dollar to gold, and most other countries pegged their currencies to the dollar. Nowadays, most currency values float freely, which means that their value is constantly changing in relation to other currencies. For example, if the US dollar bought 100 Japanese yen yesterday and 105 yen today, we would say that the dollar has *appreciated* in value against the yen. There are always two sides of the coin, so to speak—if the dollar is appreciating against the yen, then the yen is simultaneously *depreciating* against the dollar. When the US dollar appreciates against the Mexican peso, US dollars have more buying power in Mexico, making Mexican goods cheaper for US buyers. Likewise, when the US dollar depreciates against the Mexican peso, Mexican goods become more expensive for US buyers.

You might think that a country would always want its currency to be stronger than other countries' currencies, but that's not necessarily the case. In fact, China is often criticized for intentionally devaluing its currency, the renminbi. Why would China deliberately lower the value of the renminbi? China's

Currency manipulation has been key to China's success in today's free international market.

TRADE BARRIERS

A *trade barrier* is any kind of government policy that blocks or restricts free international trade. There are different kinds of trade barriers.

- A *tariff* is a tax that an importer pays on imported goods. Tariffs are among the more common trade barriers. A tariff may be imposed on all imports across the board, or it may apply only to certain goods. A tariff on a specific good (for example, wine imported from France) benefits domestic producers of that good (vintners in the Napa Valley of California), but at the expense of the good's domestic consumers, since the price of the imported good (French chardonnay) will be higher than it would be without the tariff, and thus higher than a comparable domestic version of the good (Napa Valley chardonnay). Another possibility is that the tariff will reduce the quality and variety of domestic versions of the good (chardonnay produced in the Napa Valley as well as chardonnay produced in Oregon and the state of Washington) because the tariff means that domestic producers of the good will probably have less competition from foreign producers.

- *Import quotas* are limits on the amount of a good that can be imported. The United States has used import quotas to protect a number of domestic industries, including the sugar industry, the tobacco industry, and industries producing other agricultural goods.

- *Voluntary export restraints (VERs)* are similar to import quotas with respect to their economic impact, but they're not exactly imposed by the importing country. They're voluntary in the sense that the exporting nation imposes the restraints on itself, but it typically does so in response to political pressure from the importing country.

- *Quality restrictions* are just what their name implies: restrictions based on the quality of goods to be imported. For example, some nations choose not to import hormone-injected beef from the United States. Similarly, some countries choose not to import products that fail to meet certain environmental standards. The intent of this kind of regulation may be consumer safety, but restrictions based on quality do create trade barriers. At times, countries set up standards like these for the sole purpose of protecting their domestic industries without having to impose an outright tariff or quota.

- *Government subsidies* to the domestic producers of a good are often viewed as a trade barrier. For example, if the government of one country pays subsidies to its producers of solar panels, then another country's producers of solar panels who don't receive government subsidies will find it hard to compete with the subsidized producers, since the unsubsidized producers will have higher costs.

- An *embargo*, typically imposed for political reasons and not for the purpose of protecting domestic firms and industries, is a complete ban on trade with a particular nation. A well-known example is the long-standing embargo that the United States imposed on trade with Cuba.

economy relies heavily on the export of Chinese goods to other nations. When the value of China's currency is low—that is, when a US importer's dollars can buy more units of a television imported from China—the importer passes the savings on to US buyers, who pay a comparatively low price for the Chinese TV. So where does the criticism come in? Some analysts characterize China's currency manipulation as a form of trade protection—since Chinese goods are less expensive for foreign buyers, goods produced outside China will be more expensive for Chinese buyers, a situation that discourages foreign producers of goods from exporting their products to China for sale to Chinese buyers.

FREE TRADE AGREEMENTS AND OTHER FORMS OF ECONOMIC INTEGRATION

Thanks to international trade, we have access to goods from all over the world. In addition, competition from foreign producers keeps our domestic producers on their toes. Domestic firms must strive to produce high-quality products in an efficient manner, and they must offer those products at prices that consumers are willing to pay.

Free international trade has proved so beneficial that the majority of the world's nations have entered into **free trade agreements** with other nations. Over the past two to three decades, the world has experienced a surge in the number of free trade agreements.

A free trade agreement is an arrangement among two or more nations to form what's known as a **free trade area**. The participating countries agree to reduce or eliminate tariffs and other trade barriers on the goods that they trade among themselves while keeping trade barriers in place with countries that aren't parties to the agreement. Examples of free trade agreements include the Latin American Integration Association (LAIA), which involves 14 Latin American countries, and the South Pacific Regional Trade and Economic Cooperation Agreement or SPARTECA, whose participants are Australia, New Zealand, and a number of small South Pacific nations. One of the best-known free trade agreements in the United States is the North American Free Trade Agreement (NAFTA), whose participants are the United States, Mexico, and Canada.

In addition to free trade agreements, nations may form **customs unions**, **common markets**, and **economic unions**.

- Customs unions are like free trade agreements, but the participating countries also agree to adopt a common *external tariff*.

- Common markets feature even greater integration as well as free movement of capital and labor across international borders. A well-known common market is the Common Market of the South (MERCOSUR), which was initially established by the South

American nations of Brazil, Argentina, Uruguay, and Paraguay.

- Economic unions include all the integration involved in common markets in addition to unity where certain economic policies are concerned. The European Union (EU) is the best-known example of an economic union.

The Flag of Europe was originally created in 1955 to represent the Council of Europe, but has since been adopted by the European Union and the countries belonging to its economic eurozone.

PROTECTIONISM: THE FLIP SIDE OF FREE TRADE

It's fair to say that no country has entirely opened up all its markets to competition from all the other nations of the world. For example, the United States certainly trades more freely with some nations than it does with others. Why, then, if free trade across international borders is so great, are some markets protected from global competition?

Sometimes free trade is restricted for geopolitical reasons. One country may choose not

WHAT ABOUT NAFTA?

In 1994, US President Bill Clinton, Mexican President Carlos Salinas, and Canadian Prime Minister Jean Chrétien put the North American Free Trade Agreement (NAFTA) into effect. Since then, trade has grown substantially among the three partner nations. The economies of all three have also grown.

It's to be expected, of course, that some individuals in some industries will feel a degree of pain because of this kind of free trade deal. For example, as US trade expands, US workers will probably lose their jobs if they work in an industry—say, toolbox manufacturing—in which the United States doesn't have a comparative advantage over its trading partners. Thus, with NAFTA in effect, and with trade barriers reduced, a US toolbox factory probably won't be able to compete with a Mexican toolbox factory, because Mexican-made toolboxes will be significantly lower in price because Mexican labor is less expensive. In other words, Mexico has a comparative advantage in low-skilled, labor-intensive manufacturing.

In theory, however, a trade deal like NAFTA should lead to increased prosperity for all the nations involved, at least on a net basis. Although there's disagreement among experts about how successful NAFTA has been overall, many economists believe that when a nation's whole society is taken into account, the benefits that most people gain from an agreement like NAFTA outweigh the costs to displaced workers in industries that can't compete with their comparatively advantaged trade partners. Many economists also believe that the partners to a trade agreement will benefit over time as they continue to reduce and eliminate trade barriers among themselves.

to trade with another because the two nations are political enemies. Geopolitical differences of opinion aren't the primary explanation for trade barriers, however. Some trade barriers exist because a country wants to preserve a certain aspect of its cultural identity, which means that it doesn't want foreign products—and, by extension, foreign culture—to overtake its own culture.

But that tendency doesn't explain most of the protectionism that occurs around the world. Most trade barriers are erected because of political pressure from domestic producers who want to lessen competition from foreign producers. The most common rationales for such trade barriers include arguments that a barrier is necessary to protect a so-called **infant industry**, that a barrier is necessary for national defense, that a barrier should be used as a retaliatory measure, or that a barrier will protect domestic jobs.

An infant industry is one that's new and still in development. When companies become large and produce at a large level of output, they're able to enjoy a degree of economic efficiency and cost savings called

economies of scale. The infant industry argument is that new firms need protection from foreign competition until they're large enough to experience economies of scale. Once they achieve significant economies of scale, this argument goes, they'll be able to lower their prices to the point where they'll be competitive in the global market. The problem with this argument is that, from a political standpoint, protective measures are often difficult to remove once they're in place. Also, from the standpoint of economic efficiency, protectionist measures like tariffs are usually not the best approach to propping up an infant domestic industry. Many economists would argue that direct subsidies to an infant industry would be more efficient (although the subsidies would create a whole new set of distortions in the market).

There is some merit to the argument that trade barriers are necessary for national defense, but this argument has also been abused at times. It's obvious why the United States might not want to give up the production of jet fighters. Even if another country, such as China, had a comparative advantage in jet fighter production, the US would want to keep that production at home for purposes of national security. But if we're talking about things like scissors and shears rather than jet fighters, tanks, machine guns, and other war materiel, does this argument still make sense? Probably not, but manufacturers of scissors and shears have actually attempted to secure trade protection for

their industry on the grounds that scissors and shears are vital to national security.

The argument for trade barriers as a form of retaliation—the "tit-for-tat" argument—rests on the idea that if a country imposes trade barriers on us, we should strike back by imposing trade barriers on that country. Related to this idea are the notions that some countries trade unfairly or that their production techniques violate basic human rights (e.g., they use slave labor or child labor, or their people work in sweatshops), and so we shouldn't feel too bad about punishing those countries with tariffs and quotas. But the problem with a tit-for-tat strategy is that it ends up harming domestic consumers by denying them the benefits of free trade. Situations involving human rights violations are unfortunate, but there is an argument that there are better ways to deal with such abuses than trade policy. Regardless, there will probably always be some trade barriers used for retaliatory purposes.

The argument that is probably used most often in favor of trade barriers is that they save jobs at home. Labor unions make this argument, of course. Much of the general population agrees with it, too, or at least with the notion that we're losing too many of our jobs to foreign nations. But are we really losing jobs abroad because of free trade? Certainly, but not as many as people often believe. Technological changes have played a much larger role in transforming our domestic labor markets than free trade has, and most of the jobs

we export abroad are low-skilled to no-skilled jobs, which go to countries that have a comparative advantage in production requiring low-skilled labor. The pain is intense, of course, for those people who have lost factory jobs because their companies moved their production facilities abroad. People in that situation are bound to feel anger and resentment toward the government for pursuing free trade and entering into agreements like NAFTA. Still, protectionist measures like tariffs and quotas won't do anything to prevent job losses that are brought about by technological change.

POSSIBLE DOWNSIDES OF GLOBALIZATION

As we've seen, when trade opens up across borders, there are bound to be winners and losers in the domestic economy. But as economic theory suggests, and as most economists agree, the total benefit for the domestic economy is likely to be greater than the total cost. In addition, when a country allows foreign investment inside its borders, most economic analysts also see this as a positive step.

Labor mobility—that is, the movement of workers across borders to where the jobs are— is a good thing, at least from the standpoint of

A factory in Philadelphia, circa 1925. While much industrial work that once existed in the United States has been exported abroad, more jobs have been lost in the last century to technological advancements.

economic efficiency, even though inflows of foreign workers may have adverse effects on domestic workers in certain sectors. Critics also point to other possible downsides of globalization. These antiglobalization arguments are valid, in some respects, but globalization's potential downsides have to be weighed against its benefits.

Promotion of Income Inequality

According to its critics, globalization leads to income inequality. Economic theory suggests that international trade should have an equalizing effect on income over time, but empirical studies have produced mixed results. It seems likely that the question of whether globalization promotes economic equality or inequality will depend on the countries doing the trading and on the sorts of goods they are trading.

Corporate Tax Evasion

Critics of globalization say that it promotes tax evasion on the part of multinational firms. It probably goes without saying that globalization has allowed modern corporations to adopt various tax strategies that have never been available before. Capital, whether financial capital or physical capital, tends to move to where it will bring the highest returns, and lower taxes generally imply higher returns. But cross-border tax abuse by US corporations is kept in check by the efforts of the US Internal Revenue Service (IRS) and its major counterparts in foreign countries. In addition, the Joint International Tax Shelter Information & Collaboration (JITSIC) Network has initiated systems for sharing taxpayers' information across international borders to crack down on tax evasion.

Abuse of Weaker Nations by More Powerful Nations

Globalization's critics claim that it leads to abuse of weaker nations by stronger ones. The example that critics sometimes cite is the issue of international negative externalities (see page 52 for more on externalities). It's true that the United States and some other nations ship certain kinds of waste to poorer countries—for a fee, of course—because the countries accepting the waste have less strict environmental standards for waste disposal. A prime example is e-waste, which produces highly toxic residue if not disposed of properly. According to the United Nations, "80 percent of the 2.6 million tons of e-waste that the US produces annually is shipped to Asia and Africa . . . In Guiyu, China, one of the main recipients of global e-waste, children under the age of six have an 81 percent incidence rate of lead poisoning . . . The water is so toxic in Guiyu that residents must drink bottled water. However, toxic water is still used for bathing and cleaning due to the prohibitive cost of bottled water for these activities." When abuses do occur, they do so under the guise of regular international trade. But, just as trade barriers are not the best way to deal with forced labor and other abuses of human rights, it's better to establish policies that target specific abuses of weaker nations by stronger ones, rather than attempting to tackle such abuses through broad protectionist policies that oppose globalization as a whole.

Homogenization of National Cultures

Critics of globalization see it as having led to a homogenization of cultures, with loss of cultural identity in some countries. This isn't primarily an economic argument, but it's worth considering. Globalization has undoubtedly caused some homogenization of world cultures, just as the proliferation of television across the United States homogenized our country's regional cultures in many ways. Some aspects of Western culture, and specifically some aspects of US culture, have taken root in less developed countries, but aspects of virtually every other national culture in the world have also worked their way into American life. The fear that local cultures will dissipate or disappear is not unfounded, but it has to be balanced against the benefits that societies gain from the cultural cross-pollination that has accompanied globalization.

Critics point to the lack of regulation, for example weak environmental standards, as one of the downfalls of globalization.

THE ECONOMICS OF IMMIGRATION

Anyone watching the run-up to the 2016 US presidential campaign couldn't help noticing how some candidates pushed the topic of immigration center stage. Immigration has been a hot-button issue for a long time in the United States. In fact, plenty of sound and fury about immigration (occasionally punctuated by a few facts) is produced across the political spectrum. Most of the arguments we hear about immigration have a moral or legal basis, but here are a few things that economic studies have to say about the topic:

- Numerous economic studies of immigration have been conducted over the years and, although the results aren't in complete agreement, some general patterns have emerged. A 2012 study from the Cato Institute (a free market think tank) found that liberalizing immigration in the same manner Reagan did in 1986 would add $1.5 trillion to the United States GDP over 10 years. The same study found that mass deportation of illegal immigrants would lower the country's GDP by $2.6 trillion.

- Some immigrants create businesses that employ others and add to GDP growth. In fact, immigrants to the United States tend to start businesses at a much higher rate than the US-born population, and they're responsible for a disproportionately high share of new patent applications.

- Contrary to negative stereotypes, immigrants don't simply take existing jobs. A 2011 study from the American Enterprise Institute (a pro-business, center-right think tank) found that immigrants with advanced degrees increase employment for US-born citizens. They create jobs that can pay enough to raise overall income for workers in certain fields, especially science, technology, engineering, and mathematics (the so-called STEM fields). AEI analysis also found that immigrants with advanced degrees pay significantly more in taxes than what their families receive in the way of public benefits.

- The same study also found that states with more temporary workers, both skilled and unskilled, experienced higher rates of employment among native workers. The study produced no evidence that immigration reduces the overall level of jobs for US natives, even when it included the presence of unauthorized workers.

- Giovanni Peri, an economist at University of California, Davis, found

(Opposite) Mexican immigrants entering the United States in El Paso, Texas, circa 1938. Though many see immigrants as a drain, the economic fact is that immigration has always been central to US economic growth, particularly by contributing to the country's tax base.

that immigration to the United States has actually led to wage increases for US natives. According to Peri, from 1990 to 2007 total immigration caused real income to go up from 3.3 percent to 9.9 percent per worker.

Other studies tend to support these results. Immigration does not appear to harm the economy, and in some ways it actually helps it. In addition to boosting economic output and employment, immigration also helps the economy in another important way. Our native-born labor force has been shrinking—and will continue to shrink—relative to the number of retirees receiving Social Security benefits. A similar population problem is occurring in many developed nations in the world, but the problem is especially severe in countries that are more closed off to immigration, such as Japan. (See page 147 for more on the shortfall facing the US Social Security system.) Whether you believe globalization offers more benefits to society or causes more harm to it, there's probably nothing that we can do to stop it. The economic benefits of globalization are too great and will continue to be vast. There's no doubt that as communication and transportation continue to become cheaper and faster, and as the cultures of the world continue to blend together, the world will just keep growing smaller and smaller.

1824

The Tariff of 1824

Congress passes a series of tariffs on imported or exported goods such as glass, iron, and wool in order to encourage American manufacturing, as well as to level competition from Great Britain.

1930

Smoot-Hawley Tariff Act

Originally drafted to protect American farmers from competing agricultural industries abroad, the law goes on to impose tariffs on a number of foreign products. This eventually prompts trading partners to impose tariffs against American products. In the midst of the Great Depression, the tariffs further strained American companies.

1944

World Bank and IMF

The World Bank is created and largely spearheaded by the United States as an institution providing loans to developing countries. The International Monetary Fund (IMF) is created on similar terms as the World Bank, acting as an international pool of money from which members draw and distribute funds for economic development.

1869

Suez Canal

To facilitate international trade and provide a shortened route between Europe and Asia, the Suez Canal opens in Egypt under French control. It becomes of one the world's most heavily traveled shipping lanes.

1933

Gold Standard

Convinced by experts that the gold standard made the dollar too expensive, President Roosevelt suspends the gold standard in the United States in order to reframe the value of American currency.

1948

European Union

Following two devastating world wars, The Treaty of Brussels is signed to foster cooperation between European countries leading to the eventual creation of the European Union (EU). In 1999, the euro is created as a form of currency between member states, with the exception of the United Kingdom and Denmark.

1960

Cuba Embargo

In response to the nationalization of US-owned oil refineries in Cuba, President Eisenhower outlaws significant trade between the two countries, which President Kennedy later extends.

1944

Bretton Woods System

To rebuild the world's economic relations while World War II was still ongoing, a set of money management rules among the United States, Western Europe, Australia, Asia, and Japan, called the Bretton Woods System, is established at the United Nations Monetary and Financial Conference.

1950

Prebisch-Singer Hypothesis

Raul Prebisch and Hans Singer argue that developing countries do not benefit from globalization because of the unequal trade balance. These countries tend to export commodities, but import manufactured and capital goods—and commodity prices often deteriorate in the long-term.

1994

NAFTA

North American Free Trade Agreement (NAFTA) between Canada, the United States, and Mexico is designed to make the North American countries' products more competitive at lesser costs. Each participant is granted a most favored nation status.

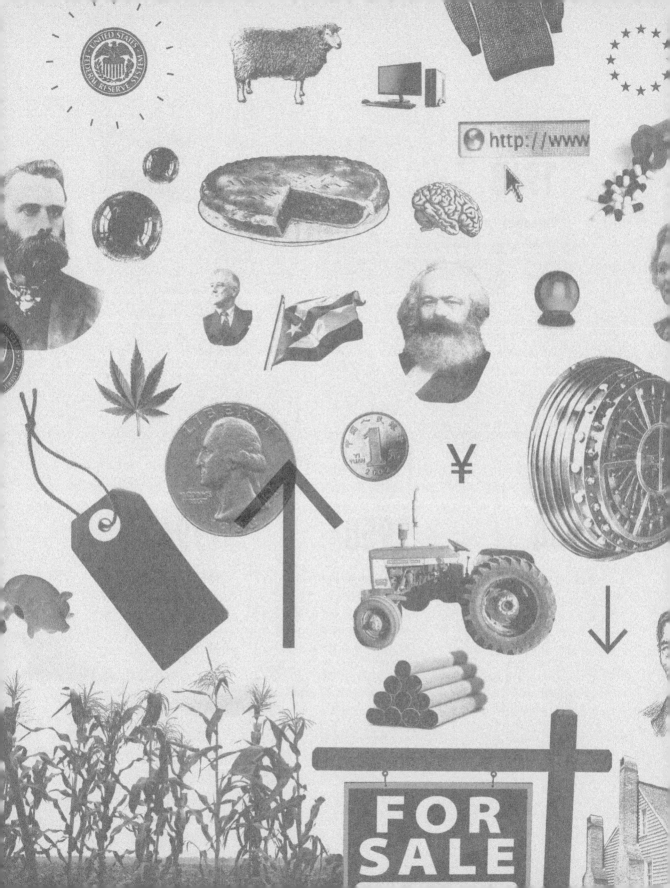

6 UNDERSTANDING THE MACROECONOMIC NEWS

Every day brings a barrage of news related to the economy, or aspects of it. Some people don't notice such news, while others follow it religiously. Most people pick up dribs and drabs of information about the economy and do their best to make sense of it. News about the economy can include lots of minute details that usually fly over the heads of non-MBA types, but much of the economic news is useful and relatively easy to understand for anyone who has learned some basic definitions and concepts. This chapter explains the differences between macroeconomics and microeconomics and discusses several measures that economists and policymakers use to gauge the health of the economy. In addition, the chapter covers the basic workings of monetary policy, fiscal policy, and the Federal Reserve.

MACROECONOMICS AND MICROECONOMICS

It's helpful to start with an understanding of the difference between **macroeconomics** and **microeconomics**. When economists talk about macroeconomics or the macroeconomy, they're referring to the economy as a whole or to the economy's larger sectors. These latter include the public sector and the private sector, which in turn is sometimes subdivided into the business sector and the household sector. By contrast, when economists talk about microeconomics or the microeconomy, they're referring to specific industries or to individual decision-making units, such as consumers, firms, or government agencies. A news story about the unemployment rate and inflation would be a macroeconomic story. A story about an auto plant shutting down in Wentzville, Missouri, would be a microeconomic story.

It's not always easy to draw the line between macroeconomic and microeconomic issues.

For example, what if the price of a barrel of oil suddenly were to rise 300 percent? The petroleum industry is an individual industry, and so when the price of a barrel of oil changes, that's clearly a microeconomic issue. But because virtually every other industry uses petroleum, a sudden spike in the price of oil would certainly affect the overall economy, and that would be a macroeconomic issue. Examining the factors that caused the price spike would mean exploring microeconomic questions; examining how that price change is affecting the national or world economy would mean exploring macroeconomic questions.

Shifts in oil prices, while industry-specific, also have a macroeconomic impact because so many other markets are dependent on oil.

INDICATORS OF ECONOMIC HEALTH

Most news related to the macroeconomy is focused on indicators of economic health. Four indicators in particular are closely followed:

- Rate of economic growth
- Unemployment rate
- Rate of inflation
- Interest rate

If we know the status of these four basic indicators for a nation, then we know a lot about the state of that nation's economy.

Rate of Economic Growth

Gross domestic product (GDP) is the primary indicator of economic growth in the US economy, although it is criticized for its shortcomings. Additional indicators include the Leading Economic Index (LEI) and the Dow Jones Industrial Average (DJIA).

Gross Domestic Product

Economic growth has to do with the rate of change in a nation's total productive output, or gross domestic product, over some period of time. GDP can be thought of as the total spending in the economy on domestically produced goods and services. (With some statistical adjustments, the total spending and the total output in a country balance out.) Gross domestic product is distinguished from gross national product (GNP), a related but different concept. Whereas GDP focuses on where production is taking place, GNP focuses on the citizenship of the people who are the owners of the factors involved in production. For example, the output of a Japanese-owned Toyota plant in Georgia would be included in US GDP because the output is occurring on American soil, but the plant's output would not be included in US GNP because the plant's owners are Japanese citizens. Instead, the output of the Georgia-based Toyota plant would be included in Japan's GNP.

GDP can rise, but it can also remain flat or even decline. People like to use a pie as a metaphor for the economy, and GDP tells you the

APPLES TO ORANGES, OR APPLES TO APPLES?

Gross domestic product isn't the only area where the nominal-versus-real concept is useful. Any monetary figures compared across time can be adjusted to produce a true apples-to-apples comparison.

An example that's relevant to everyone is nominal income versus real income. Suppose that at the end of your first year at a new job, your boss told you that you were getting a 5 percent salary increase. At first you'd be excited, but what if you learned that prices overall had gone up by 6 percent during the past year? Your *nominal* salary increase would be 5 percent, but in *real* terms your salary would actually be going down by 1 percent. It would be time for you to negotiate a new salary increase, one that took inflation—that 6 percent rise in prices—into account.

The nominal-versus-real concept also applies to interest rates. Real interest rates are interest rates that have been adjusted for inflation. Thus, when you hear commentators say that the interest rate is at 0 percent, they're referring to the real interest rate. They don't mean that you can expect to pay 0 percent interest on a loan. They mean that the lender who issued you a loan at a nominal interest rate of 6 percent last year will receive, after adjustments for inflation, a real return of 0 percent this year.

size of the pie. When the pie gets bigger, you and I can both have a larger piece without cutting into anyone else's portion. When the pie gets smaller, both of us must either accept a smaller piece or fight to keep our pieces the same size while others sacrifice.

In the United States, GDP is reported on a quarterly basis by the Commerce Department's Bureau of Economic Analysis. The rate of economic growth is represented by the percentage change in the country's GDP from one period to the next. For example, if GDP is $100 billion in year one and $105 billion in year two, then the rate of economic growth from year one to year two is 5 percent.

When the national income accountants at the Bureau of Economic Analysis calculate the rate of economic growth, they have to be careful to use **real GDP** rather than **nominal GDP** in their calculations. Real GDP is adjusted for inflation—or, to put it more broadly, real GDP is adjusted for changes in the nation's price levels. For example, suppose you want to compare US output in 1950 to US output in 2010. In 1950, nominal GDP—the unadjusted level of output—was about $300 billion. In 2010, nominal GDP was about $15 trillion. It wouldn't really be accurate to say that Americans were 50 times more productive in 2010 than in 1950, because nominal GDP for a

given year is measured in terms of that year's prices, and the prices of most goods and services have ballooned since the 1950s. For that reason, if you want to compare US output for 1950 with US output for 2010, the first thing you need to do is make adjustments for how much prices rose over that 60-year period. In this particular example, because your analysis spans six decades, you may also want to factor in the population change over that time. GDP divided by the population is known as **per capita GDP**, and it's an especially handy measure for comparing the economy of one nation to that of another.

Using GDP as a measure of the nation's economic health has its critics, and they make a number of arguments against this practice.

- *GDP accounts only for output, not for the inputs required to generate that output.* For example, GDP doesn't take into account any environmental damage that may have occurred while a year's output was being generated. Imagine that the United States wanted to boost GDP in a particular year by cutting down all the trees in all the national forests and selling the timber to our overseas trading partners. The sales of all that timber would certainly show up in GDP and would probably add billions to the final tally. But it would be difficult to argue that the country would be better off for having harvested every tree in every national forest. On those grounds, some critics

Amidst globalization, calculating a country's income can be complicated, as is the case for a car plant owned by a foreign company. Here, the share of the GNP "pie" goes to the home country.

argue that an adjustment, in the form of a subtraction, should be made to GDP to account for the nation's use of natural resources in generating domestic output.

- *GDP includes economic activity surrounding many negative events.* When a hurricane destroys a city, it brings loss and pain to the city's residents, but when contractors rebuild the city, all that construction goes into the year's GDP. Critics of GDP as a measure of economic well-being often cite the 19th-century French economist Frédéric Bastiat and what he called the *broken window fallacy.* In his theory, Bastiat disproves the idea that destruction (i.e., a broken window) and the costs of repairing it benefit society. Even though a homeowner would pay a repairman to fix the broken window, thereby increasing GDP, that home-owner now has less money to spend on other goods and services. Including the economic activity surrounding a disaster in the GDP ignores the opportunity costs of all that repair work, which necessarily precludes other kinds of productive activity.

- *GDP includes activity that involves human pain and suffering apart from the effects of natural disasters or social unrest.* For example, when an economy grows, traffic congestion tends to increase, and so does the number of traffic accidents and fatalities. For this reason, some critics argue

that GDP should be adjusted to account for traffic congestion and other negative factors.

- *GDP doesn't account for the value of non market labor.* An example of non-market labor is the unpaid housework that takes place in one's own home. Some critics argue that GDP, as a measure, has a built-in gender bias because in many

parts of the world women still perform the vast majority of domestic work.

- *GDP doesn't account for changes in the quality of products.* For critics who raise this issue, GDP's failure to account for changes in product quality is a problem because these changes are not reflected in the prices of the affected products.

- *GDP is not a good measure of a nation's level of well-being and happiness.* GDP was never intended to be a measure of human happiness, but that doesn't stop some people from equating a rise in GDP with an increase in well-being for a nation's citizens. The assumption, of course, is that people are happier when they're better off financially. Economists and other social scientists have studied happiness and discovered that money increases personal happiness only to a certain point. Maybe that's why one country uses a different measure of national economic well-being. That measure, *gross national happiness*, was adopted years ago by the Kingdom of Bhutan to signal the country's commitment to incorporating Buddhist values into its economic framework.

In 1995, a group called Redefining Progress developed an alternative measure of national economic well-being. The Genuine Progress Indicator (GPI), which is based on 26 different factors, seeks to correct the shortcomings just mentioned as well as some others. The factors that the GPI accounts for include income distribution, crime rates, public infrastructure, and so-called defensive expenditures (for example, repair bills after car accidents

Frédéric Bastiat (1801–1850), who argued against the notion that even negative events like natural disasters generate positive economic activity, was also a critic of protectionism.

or household expenditures on pollution-control devices). The GPI also includes the value of volunteer time, which doesn't appear at all in GDP.

Although per capita GDP in the United States has grown steadily and fairly significantly over the past several decades, values for the GPI over the same period have remained relatively flat. It's hard to imagine policymakers switching to the GPI as an official measure any time in the near future. GDP will probably remain the primary indicator of economic growth for a long time to come, but the GPI, as a concept, offers some interesting ideas.

The Leading Economic Index

People who watch the market are always demanding more information—as much as they can get—and so a number of indicators other than GDP are reported to help provide not only a fuller picture of the economy's performance but also clues about the direction in which the economy may be headed.

Many of those indicators are fairly easy to interpret, such as new home sales and housing starts (new construction on privately owned homes). When either of those goes up, it's good news for the economy. A complete discussion of all the economic indicators in use would take up an entire book, but one of them, the Conference Board's Leading Economic Index (LEI) deserves mention because it includes a lot of valuable underlying information and can be useful in predicting economic upturns and downturns.

The fact that it's called the Leading Economic Index doesn't mean that the LEI is in first place among economic indicators. What it means is that, as an index of *leading* economic indicators, the LEI predicts changes in the economy. The 10 key variables that the LEI tracks tend to reveal coming trends earlier than the variables that other economic indicators are watching.

On average, the LEI does a better job of predicting future economic conditions than any of its 10 underlying variables does on its own. The LEI's predictions don't always come true, of course, but they're accurate often enough that serious market watchers pay close attention to the LEI.

The Almighty Dow

The Dow Jones Industrial Average, commonly referred to simply as the Dow, is a widely reported stock market index that was created in 1896 by Charles Dow, a *Wall Street Journal* editor and cofounder of Dow Jones & Company. There are other indices reported in the media, such as the Standard & Poor's (S&P) 500 Index and the Nasdaq Composite Index (the Nasdaq, as it's now called, was originally known as NASDAQ, which stood for National Association of Securities Dealers Automated Quotations). The Dow is the

(Opposite) Charles Dow (1859–1902) cofounded The *Wall Street Journal* in 1889, making it the first publication dedicated to stock market information.

oldest stock market index and remains the most widely reported.

The Dow tracks the price movements of the stocks of 30 large, publicly traded US corporations. It's not a straight-up average of stock prices, but when the stock prices of the 30 companies rise on average, the Dow also rises.

Even though it's called the Dow Jones Industrial Average, not all the companies represented in the Dow are involved in heavy industry. The index also includes technology firms (Apple, Microsoft, IBM, Intel), financial services firms (American Express, Visa, Goldman Sachs, JPMorgan Chase), retailers (Wal-Mart, Home Depot), and entertainment and communications companies (Disney, Verizon).

The Dow is intended to give investors and market watchers an overview of market conditions and trends, but it's not without its critics, of course. Some people contend that, given the roughly 10,000 publicly traded companies in the country, the Dow uses too small a sample to provide an accurate reading of market trends.

Unemployment Rate

Economic growth is important, and not just because it alleviates the need for difficult and sometimes painful trade-offs. It's also important because it's highly correlated with job growth; when the economy grows, employment increases. That's why the unemployment rate is one of the most closely watched economic indicators. It's a true measure of well-being and provides some indication about what's really happening on the ground.

In this country, the unemployment rate is calculated by the US Department of Labor's Bureau of Labor Statistics, which takes the total number of unemployed individuals and divides that number by the total number of individuals in the labor force. For example, if there are 4 million unemployed people at a particular time and the labor force at that time consists of 100 million people, then the unemployment rate for the period of time is 4 percent.

This seems like a simple calculation, but it has two drawbacks.

- *Who is unemployed?* To be counted as unemployed for the purposes of this calculation, a person has to be actively seeking employment. If an individual loses a job, spends several months looking for a new job, and then grows discouraged and gives up the search, that individual is not counted as unemployed but is considered to be out of the labor force by choice. Even though the individual would surely prefer to be working, he or she is considered to be in the same category as someone who voluntarily chooses to stay home and care for young children.

- *Who is underemployed?* For the purposes of the government's calculation of the unemployment rate, a person who is working part-time but would prefer to be working full-time is considered to be in the same category as a person who is working full-time. Even a part-time employee who works only one hour per week is officially counted as employed. (Note that underemployment is not the situation of someone who graduated with a bachelor's degree in nuclear physics, only to end up working as a barista— underemployment, in this context, has to do with how many hours someone is working, not with whether that employee is overqualified for the job.)

When you hear the unemployment rate reported in the news, keep these two shortcomings in mind. The Bureau of Labor Statistics is well aware of them, and so it reports six different alternative measures of what is called *labor underutilization*. The most comprehensive of the alternative measures, referred to as the *U6 unemployment rate*, is designed to capture marginally attached workers as well as workers who are working part-time for economic reasons (that is, because they can't find full-time

Massive unemployment during the Great Depression of the 1930s meant long lines for a free meal in many American cities.

work). Sometimes media sources report the U6 rate, but most often the unemployment rate presented in the press has been calculated by the traditional method, shortcomings and all.

It's also worth noting that when you hear the unemployment rate in the news, it's typically the unemployment rate for the nation as a whole. However, the Bureau of Labor Statistics collects and reports employment data for every state in the union along with data for metropolitan areas. This information is rarely reported in the national media, but it reveals that the employment picture is quite variable across states and across cities. For example, the unemployment rate may be in the low single digits in some states while reaching low double digits in others. Similarly, the unemployment rate is different for people of different racial and ethnic groups, age groups, education levels, and employment types (for example, blue-collar versus white-collar workers). If you're a college student, or if you have one in your life, it may hearten you to know that the unemployment rate for college grads is significantly lower than it is for high school grads who've never attended college, just as the rate is lower for high school grads than it is for those who've dropped out of high school.

Bear in mind when you run across the unemployment rate in the press that it's a national average, and so it may not reflect what's happening with employment in the area where you live. Also remember that the unemployment rate, because of the shortcomings in how it's calculated, may not capture the true amount of labor underutilization that's occurring in your town or in the nation as a whole.

Rate of Inflation

Another important measure of the health of a nation's economy is the inflation rate. Inflation is a sustained rise in a nation's overall price level for goods and services. For inflation to occur, not every price in the economy has to rise. The presence of inflation simply means that prices on average are rising.

To take a familiar example, in the early 1980s my dad paid around $1,000 for a VCR—that's a thousand 1980 dollars! (My family wasn't rich; my dad just loved watching movies at home so much that he was willing to fork over the dough.) If he wanted to buy a new VCR today, he'd be lucky to find one anywhere (since the 1980s, technology has made not only VCRs but also video stores obsolete), but the last time a new VCR was available for purchase, it probably went for around $30 or $40. Clearly, some products, electronics in particular, have become less expensive over the years. But most goods and services—gasoline, housing, clothing, higher education, healthcare, and so on—have gone up in price quite substantially over the decades. Consider movie tickets: In 1940, people paid about a quarter to see a first-run movie. Today a movie ticket will cost you more than 30 times that much, not counting the small mortgage you'll have to take out if you want popcorn and a soda. That's inflation.

TRUE-LIFE HYPERINFLATION STORIES

If you've ever heard about someone hauling a wheelbarrow full of cash to the market to buy a loaf of bread, or about people wallpapering their houses with currency, then you've heard about hyperinflation. It's not a myth—the stories you've heard are true.

- The first hyperinflation on record occurred during the French Revolution, when the inflation rate hit 143 percent per month.

- In Germany, in 1923, inflation hit a rate of 20.9 percent per day.

- In Greece, in October 1944, inflation reached 13,800 percent. Prices that month doubled every 4.3 days.

- In Yugoslavia, in January 1994, inflation peaked at 313 million percent and led to a doubling of prices every 34 hours.

- In Zimbabwe, in November 2008, the rate of inflation reached 79 *billion* percent for the month.

- In Hungary, in 1946, during the worst month of a runaway inflation spiral, the rate of inflation hit 13.6 *quadrillion* percent (that's a number with 14 zeros). The daily rate of inflation was about 195 percent, and prices doubled every 15.6 hours. Just two years earlier, Hungary's highest denomination currency had been the 1,000 pengō note. By the middle of 1946, Hungary was printing a 100,000,000,000,000,000,000 pengō note (that's 100 *quintillion*).

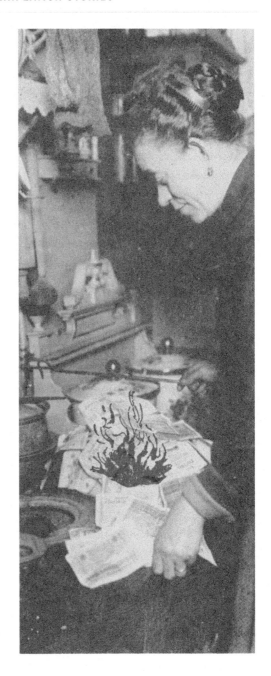

A woman in Berlin during the post-WWI hyperinflation period, when paper money was so worthless Germans preferred to use it as fuel fodder.

Most of us don't see inflation as a big problem as long as our wages are keeping up, and fortunately, wages, like prices, have gone up over the decades. The median salary in 1940 was somewhere between $800 and $1,000 annually. But inflation can become a serious problem in any economy.

- Inflation harms people who live on fixed incomes, such as income from a pension that doesn't include a cost-of-living adjustment (COLA).

- Inflation penalizes savers whose methods of investment (such as certain kinds of bonds and annuities) aren't indexed to inflation.

- Inflation harms lenders who haven't accurately factored inflation into the loans they've granted (the corollary is that unexpected inflation helps debtors, who end up repaying their loans in dollars of diminished value).

The real threat of inflation is that, left unchecked, it can get out of hand and lead to a rapidly accelerating inflation spiral known as **hyperinflation**. When hyperinflation occurs in a country, the monetary system typically breaks down. People no longer want to use the national currency, even if the government tells them to. They resort instead to using some other country's currency, or they simply barter for goods and services. Because of the serious threat that inflation can pose if it gets out of control, central banks in countries around the world keep a close watch on price levels, and sometimes a country's central bank intervenes to manage the value of the national currency. Policymakers and market watchers in the United States start to get spooked if the inflation rate gets much above 4 or 5 percent annually.

How Is Inflation Measured?

The inflation rate is calculated as the rate of change in a **price index**, which represents an average of prices for multitudes of goods and services in an economy. The best-known price index is the **consumer price index (CPI)**, which tracks price changes for several hundred goods purchased by a typical urban household. Another well-known price index, the **producer price index (PPI)**, tracks average price changes in wholesale, manufacturing, and commodities markets (as its name suggests, the PPI tracks prices paid by producers rather than those paid by consumers). When a price index like the CPI goes up over time, the economy is undergoing inflation. Both the CPI and the PPI are calculated and reported on a monthly basis.

If Prices Can Go Up, Can They Come Down?

As we've seen, the prices of some products (the VCR, for example) have gone down dramatically over the years. Those price decreases largely occurred because improvements in technology made the goods much less expensive to produce. It's also possible for overall price levels to fall. A drop in overall prices is known as **deflation**.

You might think it would be great if prices suddenly started falling for all goods and services, but deflation is generally viewed as an indicator of a troubled economy. Typically, prices fall because demand for goods and services is also falling. When goods begin piling up in warehouses, sellers have no choice but to lower prices to move the merchandise.

Deflation can also complicate things in a shrinking economy. In a deflationary environment, people may delay certain purchases because they expect prices to drop even more. If enough people hold off on making their purchases, total demand will continue to fall, and the result may be a deflationary spiral. Overall, stable prices are better for an economy than rapidly rising or falling prices.

Interest Rate

Interest is the charge paid to a bank or other lender for borrowed money—usually a certain percentage of the amount borrowed. In other words, the interest rate is the price of money.

There are many different types of interest rates in the economy. For example, there are short-term rates, intermediate-term rates, and long-term rates. There's also the **prime lending rate**, which is the interest rate that banks charge their most creditworthy customers (borrowers with credit scores that are less than perfect are charged a rate higher than the prime lending rate). And there's what's known as the **federal funds rate**, which is the interest rate that US banks pay each other for overnight loans (talk about a short-term rate!).

There's much more to say about interest rates, both as a measure of economic health and as a factor affecting the macroeconomy. We'll pursue that topic in full in the discussion presented in the following section.

MONETARY POLICY, FISCAL POLICY, AND THE FEDERAL RESERVE

Increases and decreases in the money supply, periods of recession and inflation, times of economic expansion and retraction, the rise and fall of interest rates and rates of employment— all these facets of the economy are complex and interdependent, and all of them are affected by the actions of the Federal Reserve.

Monetary and Fiscal Policy

Monetary policy is the set of actions taken by a central bank to regulate the size and growth of a nation's money supply. The money supply consists of more than just the currency and coin circulating in the economy. It also includes things like traveler's checks and deposits to checking accounts. Some measures of the money supply also include money held in savings accounts, money market mutual funds, and money market deposit accounts.

In the United States, the federal government plays a role in managing the economy and influencing the macroeconomy through its **fiscal policy**. The government tools of fiscal policy come down to two basic elements: taxes and expenditures.

- When the economy falls into recession and the unemployment rate begins to rise, the government may counteract the situation by increasing government spending or by cutting taxes. When taxes are reduced, households have more funds available to spend, and businesses have more funds to invest. Elected officials often refer to such measures as an *economic stimulus*, or you may hear a collection of such measures referred to as a *stimulus package*.

- If the problem is not recession but an overheating economy—that is, an economy in which demand for goods and services is rising more quickly than suppliers can keep up with it—the government may try to cool the economy off by reducing spending or raising taxes.

It takes time to implement fiscal policy—things don't always move quickly in the nation's capital, and even well-advised and well-intentioned measures can be held up by partisan politics and disagreements.

Is it better to cut taxes or raise spending to heal a recession? Fiscal conservatives tend to advocate tax cuts, and fiscal liberals typically argue for boosting government spending. What about when the economy is overheating? Fiscal conservatives generally prefer to cool it down by reducing government spending, whereas fiscal liberals usually advocate a tax hike. Of course, the preferences just described don't fully do justice to real-world politics, a complex arena in which conservatives and liberals are sometimes required to make compromises and trade-offs.

The Federal Reserve

In the United States, the central bank is known as the Federal Reserve, and it's often referred to simply as "the Fed." A number of important duties fall to the Fed, and we'll discuss them in a moment. First, though, let's look at how the Fed came into being and what it looks like today.

The History and Structure of the Federal Reserve

When the United States was founded, and for many decades afterward, there was great mistrust of banks in this country. From the late 1700s through the first third of the 1800s, the United States had two central banks—the First Bank of the United States (1791–1811) and the Second Bank of the United States (1816–1836)—but neither one lasted more than 20 years. The forces opposed to a central bank ultimately proved stronger than those in favor of one, and so the country operated without a central bank for most of the 1800s. Finally, after a series of bank panics in the early 20th century, a plan came together for an enduring US central bank. Congress passed the Federal Reserve Act in 1913, and the Federal Reserve System was born.

The Federal Reserve structure represents a compromise between those who wanted a strong central bank and those who feared its development. One aspect of the compromise is that the bank wasn't set up as one large institution but rather as 12 main Federal Reserve banks distributed throughout the country. Each bank is responsible for its own district, but they all work together toward the same general goals.

In addition, the 12 Federal Reserve banks, along with their branch banks, are overseen by a single body known as the Federal Reserve Board of Governors. The board's seven members are appointed by the president of the United States, and their terms are staggered so that no single president can appoint all the board members. Their terms are also fairly long—14 years—and so they are able to focus more on the long-term health of the economy than on short-term outcomes. The chair of the Federal Reserve Board of Governors invariably becomes a well-known figure in the financial world. The most famous Fed chair in recent times was Alan Greenspan. In 2014, Janet Yellen became the first woman to serve as chair.

(From left to right:) Janet Yellen, the first woman to serve as Chair of the Board of Governors of the Federal Reserve System, with former chairs Alan Greenspan, Ben S. Bernanke, and Paul A. Volcker.

WHAT IS QUANTITATIVE EASING?

In the wake of the 2007–2008 recession, a new term cropped up in the financial press in relation to the Federal Reserve: *quantitative easing (QE)*. When the Fed takes this measure, it makes large purchases of securities in an effort to boost the economy.

In a sense, QE is just a new flavor of traditional monetary policy. After all, the Fed has long participated in the government securities markets as a way to manage the money supply. But QE is somewhat different from the Fed's standard open market operations, and its introduction was controversial because it entailed a new strategy on the part of the Fed, one that some observers saw as a last-ditch effort to save a tanking economy after short-term interest rates had already fallen as far as they could.

In QE, instead of simply purchasing short-term government bonds, the Fed buys longer-term securities from commercial banks and other financial institutions. When the Fed buys these securities, their prices go up, the banks' reserves increase, and the money supply grows. Each time the Fed undertakes another round of quantitative easing, the financial press assigns it a new number—QE2, QE3, and so on—to distinguish that round from the one that preceded it.

Although the Fed's reliance on the QE strategy has raised fears of a potential spike in inflation in the future, the Fed assures the public that it has the situation under control. The jury is still out as this book goes to press—only time will tell if quantitative easing was a strategy worth pursuing.

The Federal Reserve Board of Governors, along with five presidents from among the 12 Fed banks, comprise a group called the Federal Open Market Committee (FOMC). The FOMC is one of the most powerful and widely watched governing bodies in the world. The FOMC is responsible for the nation's monetary policy, and so when any member of the FOMC speaks, people around the world stop to listen.

The Fed and Monetary Policy

One of the Fed's jobs is to manage the nation's monetary policy. This doesn't mean that it prints the nation's currency—the US Department of the Treasury handles that task—although it does release newly printed currency and freshly minted coin into the economy. Along the same lines, the Fed removes unfit currency from circulation. In addition, the agency processes a significant proportion of the checks that are cleared between banks. The Fed also serves as the federal government's fiscal agent, conducts economic research, supervises financial institutions, and acts as a bankers' bank. These are important functions, and the Fed carries them out admirably. But the most important way in which the Fed manages the nation's monetary policy is by managing the level of reserves—that is, cash deposits and other liquid assets that have been set aside—in the nation's banking system.

The Federal Reserve has three basic tools of monetary policy at its disposal. In other words, it has three different approaches available for managing the money supply:

- **Discount Rate.** Since the Fed acts as a bankers' bank, it offers loans to banks in need of reserves. The interest rate that the agency charges on such loans is known as the *discount rate,* and it's the only interest rate directly controlled by the Fed. If the agency wants to inject more reserves into the banking system, one way it can do so is by lowering the discount rate—that is, by making it cheaper for banks to borrow reserves from the Fed. Of course, there is some truth to the old saying that you can lead a horse to water but you can't make it drink—the Fed can lower the discount rate, but a bank may choose not to borrow reserves for fear that too much borrowing from the agency will trigger an examination (an evaluation of the bank's safety and soundness). For that reason, lowering the discount rate may not be the most effective tool the agency has for controlling the money supply, but it does offer a way for the Federal Open Market Committee to signal its intentions regarding the economy's interest rates.

- **Required Reserve Ratio.** The Fed establishes the *required reserve ratio.* All banks are required to keep a portion of their *outstanding deposits* in reserve, and banks that are members of the Federal Reserve System keep some of those reserves on hand at the Fed. The required reserve ratio determines the specific portion of the outstanding deposits that banks are required to set aside. For example, if a bank has $10 million in outstanding deposits and the required reserve ratio is 10 percent, then the bank is required to keep $1 million in reserve. If the agency wants to increase the reserves in the banking system, and thus increase the supply of money circulating in the economy, it can do so by lowering the required reserve ratio.

- **Open Market Operations.** The Fed engages in *open market operations*—that is, the Fed buys and sells government securities on the open market, such as US Treasury bonds and other instruments that the government uses to finance its operations. When the Fed wants to increase the money supply, it can buy government securities from banks. The Fed has to pay the banks for the securities, and the banks in turn are required to set aside a percentage of that payment in their reserves. Like this, the Fed's purchase injects reserves into the banking system. With more reserves in the banking system, the banks make more loans, the money supply increases, and interest rates fall. If the economy is overheating and the Fed wants to cool it off, it can sell government securities to banks. When the banks pay for the securities, their reserves go down. Lower reserves mean fewer loans, a situation that in turn implies a falling money supply and rising interest rates.

The Fed and Interest Rates

The Fed is also responsible for promoting growth in the US economy through low inflation and low unemployment. The Fed seeks to achieve this goal by managing the economy's interest rates.

Here are two basic points to remember:

- When the money supply goes *up*, interest rates go *down*.

- When the money supply goes *down*, interest rates go *up*.

It follows, then, that if the Fed wants to lower interest rates, it can increase the money supply. With more money available in the economy, the price of money—the interest rate—falls. If the Fed wants to raise interest rates, it can reduce the money supply. With less money available in the economy, the interest rate rises.

We've seen how the Fed can manage interest rates by controlling the money supply, but how does managing interest rates promote economic growth and keep inflation in check?

It's a relatively straightforward process, but it's also a delicate balancing act. When the Fed lowers interest rates, households tend to make more purchases on credit (houses, cars, appliances, and other big-ticket items). When money is cheaper, businesses also invest more by expanding their operations. As household and business spending goes up, the economy grows. Jobs are created, and the unemployment rate falls. This approach, called **expansionary monetary policy**, is the one that the Fed uses to fight a recession.

However, if the Fed makes too much money available for too long—that is, if interest rates remain too low for too long—then the result may be inflation. If inflation rises to an unacceptable level, the Fed can counteract the problem by raising interest rates. Higher interest rates lead to lower household spending and lower business investment, and these decreases in spending have the effect of cooling off an overheating economy and dampening inflation. This approach is referred to as **contractionary monetary policy**.

(Opposite) The Fed's approach to regulating interest rates and cash supply can determine how well or rapidly the country recovers from a financial crisis.

1791

First Bank of the United States

Congress approves the creation of a national bank in order to settle debts from the revolutionary war and build the country's credit.

1896

Dow Jones Industrial Average

Wall Street Journal editor and Dow Jones & Company cofounder, Charles Dow, creates a stock market index that calculates the average number of stock exchanges between 12 of the largest US companies.

1937

Macroeconomics, Defined

Joan Robinson is the first to define macroeconomics as the "theory of output as a whole."

1850

Broken Window Fallacy

French economist Frédéric Bastiat uses a broken window analogy to dispute the notion that wartime economies are beneficial for a nation since much of the goods produced during war are used to destroy and, in the aftermath of war, a great deal of resources are allocated toward rebuilding what is destroyed.

1913

Federal Reserve Act

Created in response to a series of financial panics that stormed the country, the Federal Reserve is created to advance employment, stabilize prices, and moderate long-term interest rates.

1934

Gross Domestic Product

The GDP, or the estimated value of all goods and services produced in a fiscal year, is first used as a measurement of a nation's economic strength in a report to Congress. Ten years later, it becomes a standard way of analyzing economies.

1971

Nasdaq Opens

The National Association of Security Dealers Automated Quotations serves as the first electronic stock quotation system. Eventually, the Association provides investors with options for trade, which were done mostly by telephone.

2008

Zimbabwe Inflation

After years of currency devaluation in Zimbabwe, hyperinflation reaches an all-time high of 11.2 million percent, according to official records. In effect, the Zimbabwean government is forced to print larger and larger sums of money at a devastatingly unsustainable rate.

1943

Emergency Price Control Act

By issue of an executive order, President Roosevelt freezes rent prices across the country in order to prevent inflation during a fully employed wartime economy due to US participation in World War II.

1995

Genuine Progress Indicator

Recognizing the shortcomings of the GDP to measure the well-being of a nation's economy, a group known as Redefining Progress creates an alternative measure focusing on expenditures relating to construction, crime, stress, and other phenomena related to a nation's economic development.

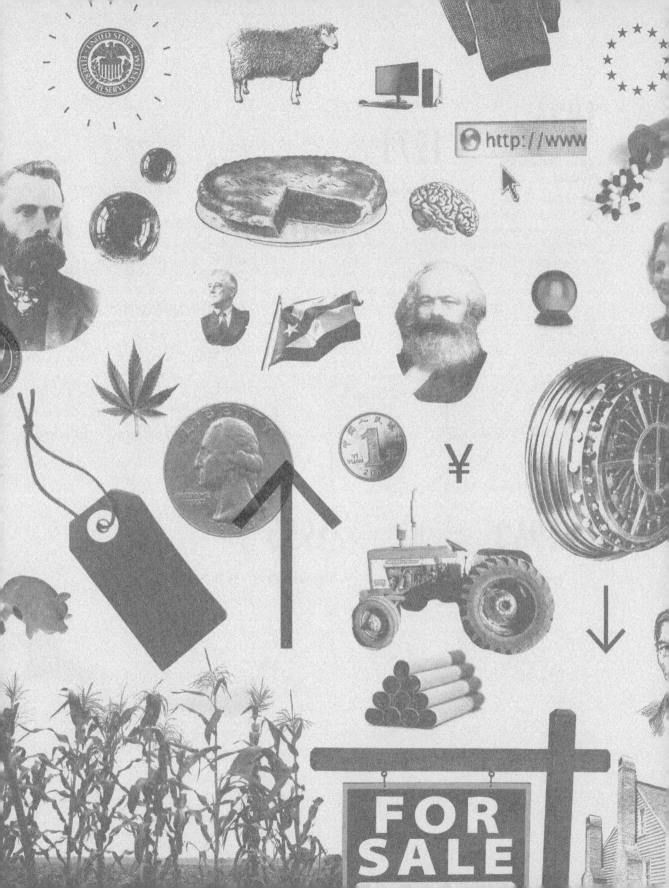

BOOMS, BUBBLES, & BUSTS

If you follow the financial news long enough, you'll inevitably hear about booms, bubbles, and busts, though not necessarily all in the same report. Most people have at least a vague idea of what these terms mean, but few understand their relevance to daily life. This chapter discusses these concepts and places them in the broader context of business cycles. This chapter also describes the phases and causes of business cycles. As part of the discussion, a few common questions are addressed. How frequent are recessions in the United States? Do recessions affect all sectors of the economy in the same manner? Could the United States ever experience another event like the Great Depression? And who is to blame for the financial crisis—the subprime mortgage crisis—that began in 2007?

THE BASICS OF BUSINESS CYCLES

During the Great Depression, the economist John Maynard Keynes referred to what he called *animal spirits,* by which he meant an unthinkingly optimistic urge to take action, as opposed to sober restraint based on mathematical realities and economic thinking. Six decades later, Alan Greenspan, former chair of the Federal Reserve Board of Governors, used another term, *irrational exuberance*—the title of a famous book by the economist and Nobel laureate Robert Shiller—to talk about the same phenomenon. We can blame animal spirits, irrational exuberance, or the bogeyman for that matter, but booms and bubbles—and the busts that result—have been recurring features of our economy for at least as long as economic data has been recorded. The terms *boom, bubble,* and *bust* are used in the financial press because

they have a dramatic ring to them, but they belong to a broader discussion of business cycles, a discussion that uses terms that aren't nearly so dramatic.

Economic activity tends to rise and fall over time, and these fluctuations are commonly referred to as *business cycles*. The presence and phases of business cycles are typically indicated and measured by changes in real GDP over time (see page 105 for a discussion of nominal versus real GDP). A single business cycle has four basic phases:

1. At the *peak* of a business cycle, total production in the economy is temporarily maxed out (although it's possible and even likely that the economy will reach an even higher level of output at some point in the future). At the peak, unemployment is low—not at 0 percent, but as low as it can go in the current economy.

2. After the economy peaks, it goes into *recession*. Most people are familiar with that term, but not everyone understands its technical meaning. A common rule of thumb among academic economists is that a recession is indicated by two or more consecutive quarters of declining real GDP. The National Bureau of Economic Research (NBER), which determines when recessions have occurred in the United States, doesn't subscribe to that principle. Instead, the NBER's Business Cycle Dating Committee says that a recession is indicated when measurable declines in real GDP, real income, employment, industrial production, and sales (wholesale and retail) have been going on for a period of more than a few months, to the point where the economy as a whole has been affected.

3. A business cycle bottoms out at its *trough,* or low point. In the trough, real GDP is at a temporary minimum, and—unless other negative influences come into play—unemployment is at a temporary maximum.

4. The *expansion* phase of the business cycle begins just after the trough, and it entails the economy's climb toward a new peak. According to the NBER, which sees recessions as normally brief and increasingly rare, the expansion phase is the normal state of the economy. Most of the time, at least in the United States and most other developed nations, the economy is growing. In electoral politics, an economy that remains flat or grows too slowly is often seen as an indictment of the party in charge.

(Opposite) John Maynard Keynes believed that government intervention was needed to mitigate the social impact of booms and busts, giving rationale for the creation of a "welfare state."

Over longer periods, the economy cycles up and down but it follows a general upward trend. Business activity rises and falls significantly over shorter periods, but it also generally trends upward over the long run.

WHAT CAUSES BUSINESS CYCLES?

Economists have long debated what causes business cycles. They've even devoted whole conferences to it, such as the one convened in 1998 by the Federal Reserve Bank of Boston. To this day, no single answer has emerged as correct or even dominant. The short answer to the question is that we really aren't sure. Through years of observation and research, however, economists have identified two major factors that definitely influence business cycles.

- **Economic Shocks.** These are unforeseen events that affect the economy and can create fluctuations in business activity. If you were to build an economic model designed to forecast the future state of the economy, your model would not include any economic shocks because you would have no way of knowing that

they would occur. In the early 1970s, the unforeseen spike in oil prices had a negative impact on the worldwide economy. Natural disasters, which are always unforeseen, can also contribute to business cycles. But economic shocks aren't always negative. For example, the introduction of a new production technology can be viewed as an economic shock with a positive effect. In fact, throughout our nation's history, many new inventions and innovations, such as the assembly

An economic "shock" can include a seemingly innocuous technological development, such as computerization, that significantly alters production or distribution processes.

line, the computer chip, and the Internet, have impacted business cycles.

- **Monetary Policy.** Monetary policy has major potential to contribute to the formation of business cycles. Some economists and schools of economic thought hold central banks largely responsible for business cycles. In the United States, for example, the Federal Reserve is sometimes seen as having engineered recessions as a result of its efforts to keep inflation in check. However, it's worth noting that if you were to compare US economic activity before 1913 (the date when the Federal Reserve System was created) with US economic activity after 1913, you would discover that there have been fewer and milder recessions since the Fed's creation than in the decades before. The evidence suggests that the Fed, rather than causing business cycles, may have succeeded in moderating them.

Throughout the 1990s and into the first few years of the current century—the period of "irrational exuberance"—some analysts began to wonder whether the business cycle might even be dead. Then, in late 2007, along came a financial crisis to remind everyone that business cycles are alive and well, and that no one has yet come up with a satisfactory answer to the question of what causes them. Even though economists aren't sure what causes business cycles, it's worth your while to know something about them. For instance:

- If you own or manage a business, you'll find it helpful to understand how your business and industry may be affected by downturns and upswings in the economy.

- If you're a worker, you can benefit from knowing something about how business cycles affect your industry, and thus your livelihood.

CYCLICAL AND OTHER TYPES OF UNEMPLOYMENT

Not all kinds of unemployment are the same. Of all the different types of unemployment, *cyclical unemployment* is the worst.

Cyclical unemployment doesn't appear in the expansionary phase of the business cycle. It only appears in the trough or during a recession. It comes about when demand in the economy isn't sufficient to generate the jobs necessary for full employment. When cyclical unemployment is present, production that could otherwise have occurred isn't realized. That lost output is gone forever and can never be recovered. Both the government, using the tools of fiscal policy, and the Federal Reserve, using the tools of monetary policy, attempt to minimize cyclical unemployment.

Economists also talk about three other types of unemployment:

- *Seasonal unemployment*, as you might guess, occurs when seasonal workers are unemployed in the off-season. For example, people who work during the summer in a resort town are seasonally unemployed during the winter.

- *Frictional unemployment* comes about when available workers cannot be matched with available jobs. That kind of mismatch is what is meant by "friction" in the labor markets. Someone who leaves one job to look for another would be considered frictionally unemployed.

- *Structural unemployment* arises because of structural changes in the economy, such as changes in technology or in the legal environment. In the 1980s, when the airline industry was deregulated, a number of airline workers lost their jobs and became structurally unemployed. People whose jobs are replaced by new kinds of technology are also considered structurally unemployed.

The *natural rate of unemployment* is what economists define as the lowest possible rate of unemployment at any given time. Every economy, at all times, will have a certain amount of seasonal, frictional, and structural unemployment, which is why no nation will ever achieve an unemployment rate of 0 percent. The corollary is that full employment does not mean an unemployment rate of 0 percent. The natural rate of unemployment varies according to a number of factors, but for the United States it's generally believed to be about 5 percent. When a country's unemployment rate is at its natural rate, the country is said to be experiencing full employment even when some workers remain unemployed.

From a worker's point of view, of course, these designations for different types of unemployment aren't particularly useful. A worker who loses her job doesn't spend much time pondering whether she's structurally or cyclically unemployed. All she knows is that she now has no immediate source of income. Even though it's not always easy even for policymakers to know for sure whether the worker lost her job because of a downturn in the economy or because a new piece of technology replaced her, the designations are still valuable because they promote sound policy by helping decision makers understand the reasons for unemployment.

- If you're an investor, what you learn about business cycles and how they work can help you spot signs of trouble ahead (as when a company's stock price is rising much faster than its revenues and profits).

- As a citizen and a voter, what you know about business cycles can help you think about how a political party or candidate would be likely to handle a swing in the economy, and about whether you want your elected representatives to actively manage business cycles or take a hands-off approach.

An old proverb says, a little knowledge can be dangerous. When it comes to economics, however, that little bit of knowledge can be extremely valuable.

RECESSIONS AND DEPRESSIONS

Sometimes people confuse the trough of a business cycle with an economic depression, but the two are not identical. At the same time, there's no true technical distinction between a recession and a depression, which is why you'll sometimes hear economists refer to a particularly severe economic downturn as a depression, especially if it leads to double-digit unemployment. As the old economics joke has it, in a recession, your neighbors lose their jobs; in a depression, you lose yours.

Recessions in the United States

Since the end of World War II, according to the NBER, there have been 11 recessions in the United States. That may seem like a lot, but not when you consider that there were 22 recessions between 1854 (the first year for which the NBER has data) and 1945.

Not only did recessions occur more frequently in earlier times, they also tended to last longer. Want proof? The recession that started in the spring of 1865 lasted for 32 months, the one that started in the spring of 1882 went on for 38 months, and the one that started in the fall of 1873 dragged on for 65 months—22 months longer than the first contraction of the Great Depression. Now compare those recessions, along with the 43-month-long contraction at the start of the Great Depression, with the longest post–World War II US recession: the one that started in December 2007 and lasted until June 2009—a total of 18 months.

A key feature of any recession is a broad economic downturn, but a recession doesn't affect all industries and all firms in the same way. Producers of **capital goods** and **durable goods** tend to feel the effects of a recession more quickly and more deeply than producers do in other sectors of the economy. Capital goods (e.g., equipment, machinery, tools) are created to help produce other goods or services. Durable goods (e.g., cars, appliances, furniture) are purchased by consumers and are intended to last three years or longer. When the economy begins to slip into recession, businesses tend to postpone investments in new capital, and so they make do with their current facilities and equipment. Likewise, as the economy begins to decline and fears of unemployment rise, households may decide to postpone the purchase of big-ticket items like cars and appliances. In the face of recession, businesses and households may also postpone new construction projects, making the construction industry particularly susceptible to swings in the economy.

Other industries tend to remain fairly steady during economic downturns. For example, regardless of what's happening in the macroeconomy, people still need health-care services, tax services, and the services of funeral directors. There are even businesses and industries—discount retailers, second-hand stores, and some of the "sin" industries (those producing alcoholic beverages and cigarettes, for example) that actually tend to do better during a recession.

The Great Depression

Most of the people who experienced the Great Depression are no longer with us, but many of their stories remain. When local banks failed, families saw their life savings disappear. Some families lost their homes and had to move in with relatives, or they had to move into shantytowns (nicknamed Hoovervilles, after President Herbert Hoover). There are stories from people who, as children, had to search through trash bins on a nightly basis to find their supper.

Needless to say, most people who lived through the Depression were deeply affected by it. Many emerged with an ultra-cautious mind-set that they carried with them for the rest of their lives. Despite the creation of the Federal Deposit Insurance Corporation (FDIC) and the advent of FDIC insurance, some people were never again able to trust a bank to hold their money.

The Great Depression truly was "great." No economic downturn that our country has experienced since then has equaled the Depression's severity or its economic impact in terms of unemployment, falling stock prices, bank failures, personal bankruptcies, and all-around pain and suffering. Depression survivors' stories of personal calamity would fill endless volumes.

Could it happen again? Could the country be hit by another depression of that length and severity? Economically speaking, anything is possible and you can get any answer you're looking for if you poll enough economists. But most economists would agree that a repeat of the Great Depression is highly unlikely in the United States. Even the recession that followed the 2007–2008 economic crisis was tame in comparison.

"Hoovervilles," shantytowns named after President Hoover, popped up around the country during the Great Depression, including this one in the middle of New York's Central Park.

One important reason why we're not likely to experience a second depression of that magnitude is that our understanding of how the economy works has increased exponentially since the 1920s and 1930s. Back then, the government and the Fed made some serious and well-documented errors in judgment, and these mistakes deepened and extended the effects of what had begun as a recession. Some economists even see those mistakes as having created the Great Depression from what might otherwise have been a run-of-the-mill recession. Today, the government and the Fed would be less likely to make such critical errors, and in the decades since the Great Depression, the Fed has had time to fine-tune the open market operations that serve as the primary tool of its monetary policy.

In addition to our improved understanding of the economy and monetary economics, we now have a social safety net, a system of protections that mostly didn't exist during the Great Depression. Some of those protections kick in automatically when hard times hit. For example, unemployment insurance is available to those who lose their jobs in a downturn, and its benefits reach beyond the individual—even though overall spending falls as unemployment rises, it doesn't fall as much as it would if there were no unemployment insurance. The same goes for welfare programs, which were introduced on a broad scale by President Franklin D. Roosevelt in the 1930s. FDIC insurance, also established in the 1930s, helps prevent the bank runs and bank failures that were endemic in the Great Depression.

It's always possible, of course, for some unforeseen event—a plague, a devastating war, widespread natural disaster, or some other shock—to change the basic structure of our economy or some of its key components. But remember what we said about economic models: When economists make predictions about the future, they have to assume that it will bear some resemblance to the past. Given everything we've learned up to this point in our history, a repeat of the Great Depression looks like a very remote possibility.

FROM BOOM TO BUBBLE TO BUST

Some people use the terms *expansion* and *boom* fairly interchangeably, and there's actually no technical distinction between an expansion and a boom. A boom, as its name implies, is a particularly dramatic expansion, one that involves rapid growth in real GDP and, usually, rapid growth in asset prices. That's why it wouldn't really be accurate to characterize all expansions as booms. Often a boom indicates that the economy is overheating, and that suppliers of goods and services are suddenly unable to keep up with demand. That rapidly rising demand places upward pressure on prices, and predictably inflation ensues. Although the general price level is bound to rise during a boom, asset prices or prices of particular categories of assets often tick up at a faster pace than the overall price level.

When the prices of certain assets, such as stocks or real estate, aren't supported by the underlying fundamentals—the factors that determine the actual market value of those assets—it's often said that a bubble, or asset bubble, has developed (synonymous terms include *speculative bubble, market bubble,* and *price bubble*).

An economic boom is typically followed by an economic bust. During a bust, real GDP falls, unemployment rises, and any asset bubbles that have been brewing are now set to burst. When they do, the prices of the affected assets fall to more reasonable levels that are more consistent with their underlying fundamentals. Analysts often refer to such a price drop as a *market correction.*

We've certainly seen our share of booms, bubbles, and busts.

In the 1920s, despite a few economic contractions, the US economy boomed over much of the decade. Someone who was alive at that time would probably tell you that life was pretty good in what came to be known as the Roaring Twenties. But, as history tells us, it all came crashing down with the stock market in 1929.

The economic boom of the late 1990s was accompanied by the so-called dot-com bubble. Then, in early 2000, that bubble burst.

In the first decade of the 21st century a housing bubble developed, thanks to low interest rates and a giant wave of "subprime"

loans (i.e., home loans that banks and other lenders made to people who didn't qualify for the prime lending rate; see page 139).

In the summer of 2015, there was a drastic drop in the prices of Chinese stocks. It turned out that the Chinese government had created an asset bubble by reporting an inaccurate growth rate for the Chinese economy. When people finally understood the true state of the Chinese economy, they saw that the stock prices were not supported by the fundamentals, and the prices underwent a sharp correction.

THE 2007–2008 FINANCIAL CRISIS: WHO'S TO BLAME?

The financial crisis of 2007–2008 took a lot of people by surprise. Debate continues to this day over who was primarily responsible for causing the crisis, which led to a recession and near double-digit unemployment in the United States. Debate also continues over how certain matters should be handled in the future. For example, should the government bail out banks and other financial institutions that are deemed "too big to fail"? Should the government promote lending practices that lead borrowers to take on too much debt?

Entire books have been written about the crisis, but in summary it began with a housing bubble fueled by low interest rates engineered by the Fed, combined with the federal government's encouragement for almost every

American to own a home, if possible. Millions of home loans were made to "subprime" borrowers whose credit histories didn't qualify them for the amounts of the loans they took on. (Left-leaning commentators tend to blame these lending practices on greedy loan officers and the firms they worked for, whereas right-leaning commentators tend to blame the government for pushing people to buy homes when they really couldn't afford to.)

Vast numbers of home loans, including a large number of subprime loans, were sold on the secondary market by the original lenders. These loans were then bundled together, and the bundles were used to create opportunities for investors. In other words, the bundled loans were used to create *mortgage-backed securities.* The securities were seen as sound investments because they were backed by collateral—the houses on which the borrowers had taken out the mortgages. As the theory went, even if a few of the borrowers defaulted and their loans went bad, the securities that had been issued on the bundles would retain their value because most of the other loans in the bundles would still be good.

Wall Street firms began to create additional investment opportunities by issuing various kinds of *derivatives,* or financial instruments related to the mortgage-backed securities. A discussion of those esoteric instruments goes beyond the scope of this book, but it's now generally acknowledged that some of them were trouble from the start (finance mogul Warren Buffet characterized them as financial weapons of mass destruction).

Everything was fine as long as the collateral behind the securities (the homes on which borrowers, including subprime borrowers, had taken out loans) kept increasing in value. As the housing market went up and up, some borrowers used the rising value of their mortgaged homes to borrow even more money, but even those who didn't were certain that they would eventually be able to sell their homes for much more than any amount of money they had originally borrowed.

When housing prices finally reached unsustainable levels, the bubble burst, and the house of cards collapsed. Housing prices rapidly dropped by hundreds of thousands of dollars. Not only were maxed-out borrowers no longer able to use the value of their homes to secure additional loans, they now owed more than they could ever possibly recover from the sale of their homes. In fact, many were so overextended that they could no longer even afford their mortgage payments. Wave after wave of defaults began. With millions of mortgage loans going bad all at once, the value of the mortgage-backed securities came into question, and so did the value of the other financial instruments based on them.

(Opposite) The financial crisis of 2007–2008 was spurred by what was essentially the simultaneous bursting of subprime mortgage bubbles throughout the country, leading to a massive market crash.

SHOULD THE GOVERNMENT PREVENT BUSTS?

Given the often drastic consequences of economic busts, you may wonder whether the government should play a role in preventing such events.

The government certainly can attempt to smooth out business cycles by using its tools of fiscal and monetary policy. But the sad fact is that, all too frequently, government policies contribute to bubbles and busts.

By their nature, most economic events are very complex, and it wouldn't be fair in any instance to say that the government is or has been wholly responsible. However, many economists would agree that misguided government policies have played a role in many of the biggest economic calamities.

Some analysts argue that the government's efforts to manage business cycles have had such poor results that it would be best for the government to take a laissez-faire approach and simply allow markets to do their thing. Others believe that the government should indeed play a role in attempting to moderate business cycles, but even among analysts who take this view, there is significant disagreement about which policies the government should pursue to achieve this aim.

Financial institutions that were holding large volumes of bad mortgages and related instruments got into deep trouble. Many people, even those who had not defaulted on their loans, reduced their spending as their total wealth, wrapped up in the value of their homes, began to plummet. Almost overnight, banks tightened up their lending standards and reduced the volume of their lending. This meant that businesses, which often depend on their ability to borrow, spent less money and hired fewer workers. The sudden reduction in overall spending led to the recession that began in December 2007 and went on for the next 18 months.

Many lessons have been learned from the 2007–2008 financial crisis, and there are still more to be gleaned from retroactive examination of the facts.

- The Fed's low interest rates laid the foundation for a housing bubble to develop, but the low interest rates in and of themselves didn't cause the bubble.

- The fact that some mortgage companies engaged in questionable lending practices contributed to the problem, but the mortgage companies wouldn't have been able to make so many subprime loans if the money had not been so readily available, and if the government hadn't implicitly endorsed such weak lending standards.

- The esoteric financial instruments created and marketed by Wall Street firms definitely added to the problem, but there wouldn't have been so many of those instruments if there hadn't been so many subprime loans available for bundling.

- Borrowers were sometimes the targets of predatory lending, but perhaps they should have known that they were taking out bigger loans than they could afford.

Clearly, there's plenty of blame to go around for the housing bubble and the financial crisis that followed. The question of who deserves the most blame is one that will probably never have a definitive answer, at least not from anyone who tries to analyze these events objectively.

1873

The Panic of 1873

New York Stock Market crashes, leading several banks toward insolvency and setting off an economic depression.

1929

Black Tuesday

The worst trading day in the history of the New York Stock Exchange, it becomes a prelude to the erasure of billions of dollars from the American economy. The Great Depression soon begins after the stock market crash.

1933

FDIC

As a part of President Roosevelt's New Deal, the Federal Deposit Insurance Commission (FDIC) is created to encourage safe practices among the nation's banks.

1920

NBER

The National Bureau of Economic Research (NBER) is created to develop objective research on economics. Today, the organization is widely relied on for start and end dates regarding recessions in the United States.

1933

The New Deal

In response to the Great Depression, President Roosevelt introduces the New Deal, a series of state intervention policies designed to provide relief for banks and job markets across the country.

1945

Boomtime

Following World War II, the United States grows in productivity for a period of over 25 years, as technology developed during and after the war leads to the emergence of new manufacturing capabilities, agricultural methods, and the exploration of air and naval power, among other developments.

1973

Oil Embargo

OPEC cuts off oil supplies to the United States in retaliation for US support of Israel. The embargo sends oil prices soaring across the globe and exposed American dependence on foreign manufacturing.

2000

Dot-com Crash

In the wake of the Internet, companies borrowed huge sums of money to purchase market shares in the new economy. Many of these purchases were not well planned, however, resulting in substantial losses and bankruptcy filings throughout.

2008

Lehman Brothers Collapses

The investment bank files for bankruptcy, citing $639 billion in assets and $619 billion in debt. Lehman's bankruptcy filing is the largest in history, and greatly deepens panic over bank credit lines across the globe.

1996

Irrational Exuberance

Federal Reserve chair Alan Greenspan uses the term "irrational exuberance" to describe the problem of investor enthusiasm increasing asset values despite the fact that such values are based on faulty or unsustainable grounds.

2007

Subprime Mortgage Crisis

A series of massive defaults on mortgage payments following years of insider trading of risky mortgages erupts across the United States and the United Kingdom.

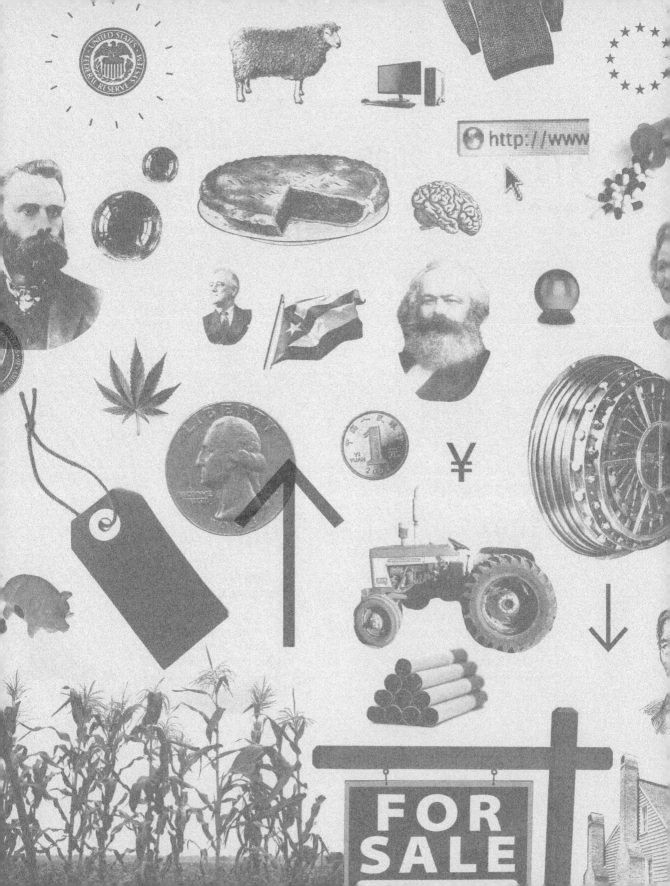

SOCIAL SECURITY, WELFARE SPENDING & HEALTHCARE IN THE UNITED STATES

A sizable share of the federal government's spending goes toward so-called entitlement programs: the Social Security program, the federal welfare program, and government-sponsored healthcare programs. Even if you're not receiving Social Security or welfare benefits, you probably pay taxes, which means that you have a stake in all of these programs. If you plan to retire one day, then you definitely have a stake in the future of the Social Security program. And whether or not you supported the passage of the Patient Protection and Affordable Care Act of 2010, you have a stake in the US healthcare system. After reading this chapter, you may modify your positions on these important issues. If you've never held a position, then this chapter will provide you with a framework that will help you formulate one.

SOCIAL SECURITY: A TICKING TIME BOMB?

Some people are convinced that the US Social Security program is doomed and that the whole thing will blow apart at some point in the next few decades. Others are more optimistic about the program's future. Which viewpoint is closer to the truth? Calling the program a time bomb is on the extreme side, but it's true that Social Security needs some adjustments to remain solvent for future generations.

The Social Security program came about under President Franklin D. Roosevelt's administration as the country was struggling to find its way out of the Great Depression. The Roosevelt administration instituted many programs in response to the Depression, but the Social Security Act of 1935 was specifically intended to help the elderly and ensure that they would have some minimum level of retirement income.

The Social Security program wasn't originally intended to provide a retiree's sole source of income, and that's still true today. The original program looked different from today's, as many changes have been made to it over the years.

- The very first benefits were one-time lump-sum payments, and they were made only to retired individuals.

- Early payments were small compared to today's payments.

- Early payments didn't automatically increase with inflation.

- In 1939, the law was changed to add survivors' benefits and benefits for a retiree's spouse and children.

- The payout of regular monthly benefits started in 1940.

- In the late 1950s, benefits for disabled individuals were added to the program.

- Beginning in the 1970s, payments were pegged to the consumer price index so that inflation would no longer erode the purchasing power of a Social Security recipient's income.

A number of smaller modifications have also been made to the program over the years, including changes to the level of taxes collected by the government to support the system.

The Social Security system worked well in the beginning, at least in terms of serving its intended purpose. Early recipients did well under the system, except perhaps those who received the earliest lump-sum payments, like Ernest Ackerman, a retired motorman in Cleveland, whose one-time payment totaled 17 cents. Apart from Mr. Ackerman and other lump-sum recipients, those who received regular monthly benefits in the early days were effectively earning an annual return of 135 percent on what they had paid into the system—in other words, for every $1 a recipient paid in, he received $1.35 in benefits. Later recipients didn't fare quite so well, but they still probably earned a higher return from the Social Society system than they would have earned from an alternative investment.

For future retirees, however, Social Security benefits won't be such a good deal. It's true that the program ran cash surpluses between 1984 and 2009, mainly because the baby boomers were in their peak earning years, but the system no longer takes in more than it pays out. The program's 2015 cash deficit is projected to be around $84 billion. According to an issue brief published by the Treasury Department, Social Security will eventually face a shortfall of $13.6 trillion in present-value terms. That $13.6 trillion represents the total amount of benefits received by previous recipients (in present-value terms) above what they paid in Social Security taxes. In theory, the Social

(Opposite) President Roosevelt signing the Social Security Act in 1935 as part of the New Deal aimed at creating a social safety net in the wake of the Great Depression.

Security Trust Fund exists, but the fund is really more of an accounting trick than a true pension fund, and it is projected to run out by 2034. Other portions of the Social Security system, such as disability insurance, are projected to be out of money much sooner. Without some action on the government's part, future Social Security recipients will face serious cuts in benefits.

The system's basic problem, and the reason why it won't work as well in the future as it did in the past, is demographics. Social Security is what's known as a pay-as-you-go system, which means that current recipients are being paid out of taxes collected from the paychecks of current workers (again, the trust fund exists only on paper). In 1945, in the system's early days, there were 42 workers to support each beneficiary. By 1960, that ratio had dropped to nine workers for every beneficiary. Today, about three workers support every beneficiary, and by 2034 the ratio will be closer to 2 to 1. The ratio has been changing for several reasons—the nation's birthrates are falling, people are living longer, and more and more baby boomers are retiring. The population is, in a word, aging.

Politicians and policymakers are aware of the problem facing Social Security. In fact, they've taken action in the past to forestall the problem. The last major set of amendments to the program, passed into law in 1983, instituted a gradual ramping up of Social Security tax rates as well as the retirement age. As the facts stand now, though, the 1983 amendments are no longer enough. Additional action is needed. Sooner or later, if no action is taken, the program will fail to meet its stated obligations.

The Myth of the Social Security Trust Fund

Many Americans believe that somewhere in Washington there's something like a bank account that contains their accumulated payroll taxes from all the years they've worked, and that this account is where their Social Security benefits will come from when they retire. It's easy to understand why so many people have this impression. Every so often, the Social Security Administration sends everyone in the United States who works or has worked a statement showing the amount they have paid in payroll taxes for each year worked. But the government hasn't stored those monies in Washington, Fort Knox, or anywhere else. The truth is that the government has already spent the money that you and I have paid into the system.

Most people already understand that the Social Security benefits paid to current recipients are funded by current workers' payroll taxes, but there's something else that many people don't realize. During the baby boomers' peak earning years (1984–2009) when the program was taking in more money than it was

(Opposite) Because the federal government spends Social Security funds on other programs as they are collected, the system is essentially an empty piggy bank.

paying out, the surplus funds were invested in us Treasury bonds. In other words, the Social Security system essentially lent the surpluses to the government, and the government used that money for many other purposes.

What we have instead of money in the Social Security Trust Fund is, in effect, a stack of IOUs. The federal government owes the Social Security Trust Fund all the money it borrowed and spent on other things. To pay the trust fund back, now that the level of Social Security benefits being paid out is higher than the level of the payroll taxes being collected, the government will have to take money away from other programs, raise taxes, or both.

So the next time you receive your statement from the Social Security Administration, remember that the payroll taxes you've put into the system over the years probably went to build a road somewhere, or fund a university research study, or finance a war, or pay a senator. The one thing that money certainly isn't doing is sitting safe and sound in a bank account until you retire.

Fixing Social Security: A Menu of Options

The Social Security problem is an interesting one for economists because it has no single, clear-cut solution. But there's a menu of possible actions that could be taken to address the problem, and they all boil down to either increasing the revenues flowing into the program, or reducing the monies paid out.

- *Raise the payroll tax rate.* This would be the most obvious way to increase the program's revenues. The tax hike would apply to all current and future workers. Because the program's financing gap gets wider as time passes, the sooner a payroll tax hike could be enacted, the sooner the gap could be closed, and the lower the tax hike could be. Conversely, the more time that goes by without a payroll tax hike, the longer it would take to close the gap, and the higher the tax hike would have to be.

- *Raise or gradually eliminate the Social Security payroll cap.* The Social Security payroll cap marks the level of income at which payroll taxes stop being collected. The cap is tied to average yearly wage growth. As this book goes to press, the payroll cap is $118,500, which means that payroll tax is assessed only on the first $118,500 of an individual's income. If the payroll cap were raised or eliminated, higher earners would pay more into the Social Security system and might also receive higher benefits in retirement. As a stand-alone measure, however, raising or eliminating the payroll cap wouldn't solve the whole problem.

- *Expand the base of workers from whom the payroll tax is collected.* Some workers, such as government employees who participate in public retirement systems, have been exempted from payroll taxes as well as from receiving Social Security benefits. Removing such exemptions would raise the Social Security program's revenues, but probably not enough to significantly reduce the program's financing shortfall.

- *Allow more legal immigrants into the country.* Our declining birthrate is one of the major causes of the Social Security problem. Workers who are legal immigrants could compensate for some or all of the deficit.

- *Reduce benefits.* Some people see an across-the-board benefits cut as the default fix: If lawmakers don't reform the program, they say, then benefits will have to be cut in the future because the money simply won't be there.

- *Raise the retirement age.* For instance, Congress could decide to declare 70 the new retirement age. That means that people under that age would see a reduction in benefits because they would have to wait until the new, higher retirement age to start receiving them.

CAN SOCIAL SECURITY BE PRIVATIZED?

Some analysts advocate privatizing Social Security, or at least some portion of it. Some proponents of privatization also recommend that individuals be allowed to decide for themselves whether they want their payroll taxes to go into the traditional Social Security Trust Fund or into market investments.

The basic argument for privatizing Social Security is that what people stand to earn from market investments will be more than any amount they would ever receive from the Social Security program. Another advantage, as privatization's supporters see it, is that a privatized Social Security program would take our already debt-burdened government off the hook for payouts to future retirees.

The basic argument against privatization is that the market can be volatile. What would happen if an individual reached retirement age just after a market crash? What if her retirement savings were totally wiped out? Would the government then step in and provide benefits for her, or would she just be out of luck?

Given this kind of risk, it's hard to imagine lawmakers ever adopting a purely market-based approach to retirement security. Yet the idea of privatization does have some merit, and it could provide a partial solution to the Social Security problem.

Younger workers could be given the option of directing part of their payroll tax monies into market investments, with the rest going into the traditional program as a backup. Such a plan might even encourage workers to save and invest at levels beyond the mandated amount represented by the payroll tax. Requiring people to make decisions about their retirement savings on something like a yearly basis would also get them actively involved in planning for retirement. Those who didn't want that level of involvement could always default to the traditional program.

Even though a fully market-based retirement savings program will probably never be adopted in the United States or any other major developed nation, the idea should be included on the menu of potential fixes for Social Security. After all, the market has a very good track record of providing solutions and partial solutions to complex economic problems.

- *Introduce means testing.* All Americans, regardless of income, are currently eligible to receive benefits if they meet the age- or disability-related requirements. If means testing were implemented, however, wealthier individuals would no longer receive benefits (of course, policymakers would have to determine the level of income and other resources that would qualify an individual as wealthy). Opponents of means testing argue that the Social Security system represents a guarantee from the government, and that the terms of the agreement make benefits available to everyone, not just to poor and middle-class retirees. In any case, means testing, like tinkering with the payroll cap, probably wouldn't work as a stand-alone measure to close the Social Security financing gap unless the cutoff for receiving benefits were set at a fairly low level.

- *Privatize the Social Security program.* Essentially, this solution means directing funds collected through the payroll tax into market investments instead of into the Social Security Trust Fund (that is, the government's coffers).

Each of these potential fixes has advantages and disadvantages, but one disadvantage they have in common is that they're all unpopular. Some seem a bit less unpopular than others, but none of them will win any points for politicians who propose them. That's another reason why the problem with Social Security has persisted—Social Security has been called the "third rail" of American politics because, metaphorically speaking, politicians who touch on this subject experience the same effect they would had they touched the electrified rail that runs along a subway track.

If you feel like running a social experiment, the next time you get together with people who like to debate politics and current events, try bringing up the Social Security problem. Lay out the potential fixes we've just discussed and watch what happens. In all likelihood, you'll have a lively debate on your hands, and you'll get a small taste of the challenge that politicians face around this issue. You'll likely find that:

- Older people who are close to retiring may favor hiking the payroll tax.

- Some younger people probably won't go for that solution, especially because many young people are skeptical about whether benefits will even be there for them in the future.

- A certain level of support from everyone for lifting or eliminating the payroll cap, and for implementing means testing, though those fixes on their own probably wouldn't solve the whole problem.

What you'll probably discover is that there's no single solution on which everyone can agree. Fixing Social Security in any significant way and making the program healthy will probably require some combination of the measures presented in this chapter.

The pollsters have their data and the pundits have their positions, but nothing can happen unless lawmakers summon the political courage to look directly at the Social Security problem and deal with it once and for all. If they don't, the situation will only grow worse. Failure to act on the issue today will only push the problem—and a drastically compounded problem at that—onto the backs of future generations.

THE DEBATE OVER WELFARE SPENDING IN THE UNITED STATES

From politicians to average citizens, Americans have long debated the merits of the nation's various welfare programs. Arguments for and against the programs tend to fall along political lines, with liberals generally in favor of welfare spending and conservatives generally in favor of reducing or even discontinuing welfare spending.

Economists, too, are just as likely to be divided along political lines when speaking out about welfare spending. The economics concepts most relevant to this issue are the notions of efficiency and equity, and the trade-off that typically occurs between the two.

Efficiency

Efficiency is just what it sounds like, at least to an economist: the optimal production and allocation of resources. A purely free market economy, one without government intervention, would have efficiency at its heart. Those individuals who were most productive would end up with a greater share of resources than those who were less productive.

In such a system, a high income would serve as a reward, or motivator, to get highly productive people producing even more. With highly productive people producing more, others in the economy would benefit. The economy would grow at a faster rate, more goods and services would be produced, and jobs would be created. Were high producers to be penalized, typically through high income taxes, they would tend to produce less (or they would take their productive talents elsewhere). The economy would suffer, and the economic "pie" would become smaller than it otherwise would have been.

This is the case often made by those economists (and others) who oppose income redistribution. For them, "a rising tide lifts all boats" is a common refrain. Opponents of income redistribution say that if highly productive individuals were allowed to fully reap the rewards of their efforts, they would be inclined to produce more, innovate more, and boost the economy. Meanwhile, people in the middle and at the bottom of the economic ladder would benefit from all that production and innovation by having more and better job opportunities, as well as better and cheaper goods and services.

Equity

Equity has to do with fairness or equality, but there are different ways of understanding what equity and equality mean. For example, a flat income tax of 15 percent on all income earners would be equal in one sense—everyone would pay income taxes at the same rate. But someone earning $20,000 per year would feel a tax bill of $3,000 much more acutely than someone earning $1 million per year would feel a tax bill of $150,000. Some applications of the equity concept account for this type of thinking.

People in favor of income redistribution don't believe that the economy works the way opponents of redistribution think it works. People who favor redistribution believe that money and other resources in a free market system tend to accumulate at the top of the economic ladder, and that money doesn't "trickle down" as some politicians have claimed. Pro-redistribution people believe that it's the government's job to ensure equity for citizens in the middle and bottom of the economic ladder. One form of redistribution is the progressive income tax, the system that requires high earners to pay a larger proportion of their income in taxes than low earners are required to pay. Another form of income redistribution is government spending on welfare programs for poor people.

Welfare's Costs and Benefits

When it comes to welfare spending, the economic evidence is mixed, as it is for so many other controversial issues. No one can objectively say whether it's better for policymakers to focus on efficiency or on equity; that's largely a matter of political and philosophical preference. But one obvious way to look at the issue through an economic lens is to examine whether the costs of welfare are outweighed by its benefits. The total *cost* of welfare spending, many would argue, consists of more than dollar outlays. Some critics see the higher taxes needed to finance welfare spending as dampening the productive efforts of high earners.

Others argue that welfare benefits undermine the work ethic of recipients, and that economic growth suffers to the extent that welfare benefits discourage people from working. To put this idea another way, these analysts say that the economy would be growing at a faster clip if all those who are able to work would actually enter the workforce and involve themselves in productive activities.

Welfare spending's *benefits* consist not only of direct payments to recipients but also of any gains to society that can be attributed to the existence of welfare spending. Honest and reasonable people can disagree about whether welfare benefits do more harm than good to an individual or a family in the long run, but there's no denying that US welfare programs have prevented or lessened human suffering to some degree, and reduced suffering represents a real economic benefit.

Some would also contend that welfare spending reduces the incidence of crime on the part of poor people. It's difficult to measure that kind of cause-and-effect relationship, but it's reasonable to assume that some amount of crime reduction can be attributed to the existence of welfare spending, and reductions in crime also have to be counted as an economic benefit.

People stand in line at a Baltimore welfare office in 1975. Some economists believe that welfare spending can serve the important role of lessening income inequality.

INCOME INEQUALITY AND REDISTRIBUTION

To measure income inequality, economists most often use *income quintiles* and the *Gini index* (also called the *Gini coefficient* or the *Gini ratio*, it's named for its creator, the Italian statistician and sociologist Corrado Gini). On the basis of these two commonly used measures, a politician or a political activist would be justified in saying that the distribution of income is becoming less equal in the United States, as in many other places around the world.

Quintiles divide a data set into five parts, and so quintiles based on income divide the population into five different income groups: the top 20 percent of income earners, the second highest 20 percent of income earners, and so on. In the United States, over the decades, the share of

income going to the highest quintile has ticked up somewhat, and the share going to the bottom earners has declined. In 2014, the top quintile in the United States earned more than 50 percent of all income, and the lowest quintile earned just a little more than 3 percent of all income.

The Gini index yields a value somewhere between 0 and 1. The closer a country is to 0 on the Gini index, the more equal its income distribution; the closer a country is to 1, the less equal its income distribution. In 1967, the United States was at 0.362 on the Gini index; in 2014, it was at 0.464, which means that our country scores among the most unequal of all the developed countries on this measure of income equality. According to a report by the International Monetary Fund, it's estimated

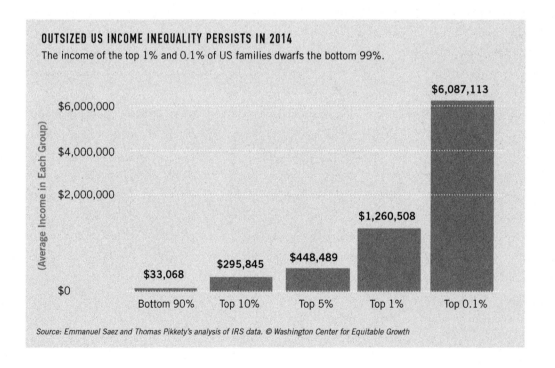

OUTSIZED US INCOME INEQUALITY PERSISTS IN 2014
The income of the top 1% and 0.1% of US families dwarfs the bottom 99%.

Source: Emmanuel Saez and Thomas Pikkety's analysis of IRS data. © Washington Center for Equitable Growth

that nearly half of the world's wealth is now held by just 1 percent of the world's population. In the United States, the richest 20 percent of people hold about 89 percent of all the wealth.

But income inequality, like all other economic issues, is complex, and there's more to the story than might be perceived at first glance.

One issue is that the common measures of income inequality have some shortcomings. For example, most of them don't include so-called "in-kind" transfers from the government, such as Medicaid, Medicare, and food stamps. When that spending is counted as income for the beneficiaries, income inequality begins to look a bit less extreme.

Another issue is that these measures offer only a snapshot of what's happening at one moment in time. They don't really tell us how income has been changing among various groups and individuals over a longer period. Between 1996 and 2005, for example, there was substantial movement among income quintiles in the United States, with 50 percent of the people who were in the bottom quintile in 1996 moving to a higher quintile by 2005, and 5 percent even making it to the highest-earning quintile. In addition, more than 50 percent of those who started out in the top quintile in 1996 had fallen into a lower quintile by 2005. To take another example, people are usually in the lower-income quintiles when they're young and first earning a living, but as they grow older and gain skills and experience, they tend to progress into higher-income quintiles. Over longer periods of time, income ends up looking more evenly distributed than it does at any given point in time.

Some economists would also point out that even if income is less equally distributed in the United States than it was, say, 50 years ago, the overall standard of living has gone up. A large proportion of today's low-income Americans own cars, cell phones, flat-screen TVs, and other such items. In many respects, it's probably not as bad to be in the bottom quintile of income earners in 2015 as it was to be in the bottom quintile back in 1965. This is not to suggest that people living in poverty should take comfort in knowing that poor people probably had it worse 50 years ago.

Some politicians and pundits would argue that we've gone too far in redistributing income. After all, too much income redistribution could dissuade the productive from producing, and that reduction in their productivity would have a negative impact on the country's rate of economic growth. By contrast, others would argue that we need to do much more to level things out.

Economists have done a good job teeing up the debate on income inequality. Ultimately, however, voters will have to decide what's fair with respect to income redistribution.

(Opposite) The concentration of extreme wealth at the top tier of US society has made it one of the most unequal developed countries in the world, confirmed by the country's Gini index rating.

A less tangible benefit, but one worth considering, is the possibility that some people who have never received or even qualified for welfare benefits still take some comfort in the knowledge that the benefits are available if the need should arise.

Welfare spending's greatest benefit may be its potential to lessen income inequality. Income inequality, which crops up more and more frequently in the media, is almost always presented as a growing area of concern for the nation. Welfare spending is a big part of income redistribution and because it may help mitigate income inequality, society stands to gain in at least two ways:

- Many people find value in feeling that they live in a country that is becoming more socially just, and when concerns about income inequality are eased by increased welfare spending, we're better off as a society.

- Some analysts argue that a high degree of income inequality may reduce a country's rate of economic growth. Reducing income inequality would therefore benefit a country's rate of economic growth.

On one hand, welfare spending may reduce a nation's economic growth rate—welfare spending may diminish the incentives for recipients to work, and the taxes that fund the programs may have a dampening effect on the productivity of people earning higher incomes.

On the other hand, welfare spending may help boost economic growth, at least to the extent that it alleviates income inequality (and to the extent that some economists are correct when they argue that greater income equality leads to higher growth).

The net effect of all of these factors is unknown at this time, but currently politicians believe that the funds spent on welfare programs are justified. Much to the chagrin of some political factions, it's unlikely that we'll ever totally eliminate welfare spending in the United States. If history is a good predictor, then the nation's total amount of welfare spending will gradually increase, and this means that the debate is not over.

HEALTHCARE: A MARKET LIKE NO OTHER

The healthcare market is so complex and challenging for economists that it has become a subfield of its own in economics. For an industry to warrant having its own branch of economics, it must be a very important industry with characteristics that make it different from typical industries. What is it that makes the healthcare market so different from other markets?

- The healthcare industry is one of the nation's most heavily regulated industries; the same is true in most nations, for that matter.

- The vast majority of hospitals in the United States operate on a nonprofit basis, so they pursue goals aside from profit maximization.

- The healthcare market is characterized by asymmetric information (see page 51) and having an ill-defined product since the outcome of healthcare is uncertain. When you're told that you need a particular screening, you have no way of knowing if you really need it or if someone is trying to pad a bill. And despite undergoing a battery of tests, you could leave the doctor's office unhealed.

- Because of asymmetric information and an ill-defined product, not to mention the effects of injury and illness, healthcare consumers may make less rational decisions about healthcare than they do about other products.

- Thanks to combinations of insurance premiums, co-payments, and government subsidies, consumers only rarely pay the full price for healthcare services. Only in rare situations does the healthcare market function like a typical market. But in the vast majority of situations, third-party payers (insurance companies, managed care organizations, and the government) form a wedge between consumers and producers, in effect disguising the true costs of services.

- Because the wedge between consumers and producers disguises true costs, consumers tend to overconsume healthcare services because they're not paying the full costs.

Suppose that my doctor offers me a treatment that isn't really vital, but it may improve my health just a little. The key word there is *may*. The treatment may have no effect at all; it may not improve my health one iota. Suppose further that the price of the treatment for an uninsured patient is $500. If I'm paying out of pocket for my healthcare, I'm going to think long and hard before I spend $500 on a treatment that may improve my health only marginally. If I only have to pay a $10 or $20 copayment, I'll likely go ahead with the treatment. For less than the price of a large pizza, I can take a chance that the treatment might actually improve my life. In fact, I may go ahead and sign up for every treatment my doctor has to offer. At $20 a treatment, I can afford lots of healthcare. Managed care operations, such as HMOs and PPOs, were designed to help prevent the overuse of healthcare and to keep healthcare costs down. There's evidence that they've had some success in meeting their objectives, but the wedge is still there. It's still the case that most of the time, most consumers don't pay the full price for the healthcare services they receive. That means that even with innovative, market-based approaches like managed care, healthcare is still far from being a typical kind of market.

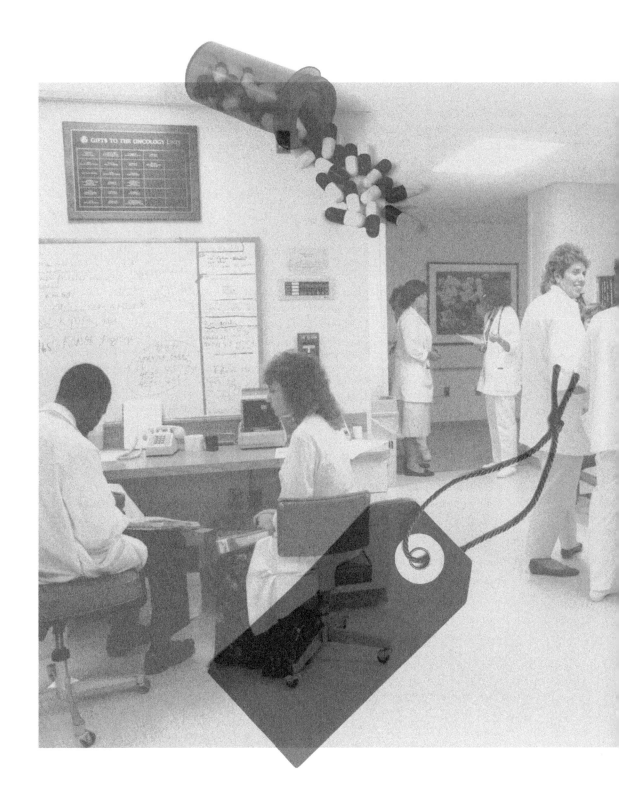

Our healthcare system is far from a pure market system, of course, since it includes government elements that operate alongside market elements. However, if healthcare is so different from other markets, it may be reasonable to ask whether healthcare should be left to the market at all. Many other advanced nations have government-provided healthcare for all citizens, and some would argue that the United States is lagging behind the rest of the developed world in this regard. People who take this position and harbor a more liberal worldview favor a system like Canada's government-run, single-payer system. That is one possible approach to healthcare.

By contrast, free market advocates argue that the government is already too involved in healthcare. Some who take this view also contend that government is the cause of the healthcare system's problems. If the government were left out of the equation, free market thinkers say, a new, market-based healthcare system would emerge that would be far superior to the one we have now.

So who's right—the free market fans, or the people who want a government-run, single-payer healthcare system? Again, not surprisingly, the issue is complex, and there's no single correct answer. Each approach has its advantages and disadvantages.

The US multipayer healthcare system involving multiple third-party insurers has created a distortion in the prices of healthcare delivery.

Should the Healthcare Market Be Given Free Rein?

If healthcare were a pure market good—that is, if people purchased all healthcare services themselves and paid the full costs directly out of pocket—overall costs might be lower. If people were spending their own money, they wouldn't spend as much on visits to doctors' offices or nonessential tests. Of course, some people wouldn't be able to pay out of pocket for all the healthcare services they needed, and that's where health insurance comes in. Yet there are several reasons why a pure market system, even a system that incorporated health insurance, wouldn't solve all the problems related to healthcare delivery.

- There would be people who couldn't afford health insurance.

- There would be people, especially young and very healthy people, who would choose not to buy health insurance even if they could afford it. That's a problem because insurance works only if there's large pool of diverse participants. If everyone in the insurance pool is old and sick, the payouts are much larger than the premiums, and the premiums become exorbitant.

- In a pure market system, insurers would have the right to accept the customers they wanted to insure and turn away the rest. Insurance companies, like other private firms, seek to maximize profits, so

DID THE AFFORDABLE CARE ACT SOLVE THE US HEALTHCARE PROBLEM?

In 2013, Australia's healthcare spending as a share of its GDP was 8.8 percent. In the same year, US spending on healthcare as a percentage of GDP was 16.4 percent, nearly twice Australia's level. US expenditures on healthcare were also significantly higher than those of the next biggest spenders, the Netherlands and Switzerland, who both spent 11.1 percent of GDP on healthcare. What do these figures have to do with the Patient Protection and Affordable Care Act (PPACA), or Affordable Care Act (ACA) for short? Just this: Before the advent of the ACA, healthcare spending in the United States was already higher than in other countries, so this isn't the reason why American healthcare is so much more expensive than other countries'. At the same time, some of the ACA's provisions may end up pushing the costs of healthcare in the United States even higher in the future.

It's not easy to find unbiased, unpoliticized information about the current status of the ACA, but so far it appears to have reduced the number of uninsured Americans, which was one of the ACA's primary purposes. There are still individuals in the United States who don't have health insurance, but millions more have acquired coverage under the ACA.

That said, it also appears that millions of Americans were kicked out of their former healthcare plans because of the ACA. Most of those people probably acquired new coverage, but President Obama's famous promise—"If you like your healthcare plan, you'll be able to keep your healthcare plan"—wasn't fulfilled.

In addition, many people's insurance premiums have gone up because of the ACA's provisions, and many more people are likely to have their premiums hiked in the future. Some people's premiums are offset by government subsidies, but not everyone is or will be subsidized. The ACA also entails a few new taxes whose impacts are still to be determined.

The architects of the ACA envisioned a network of state-run healthcare exchanges that, ideally, would allow people to buy health insurance at a lower cost than what had been available before the ACA. However, many states declined to create their own exchanges, leaving the task to the federal government, and many of the state-run exchanges that were established have struggled financially since opening for business, with some states reportedly considering turning all or parts of their exchanges over to the federal government.

As if that weren't enough, the ACA may prove to have a big unintended consequence. Under the ACA, companies that employ 50 or more full-time workers are required to provide them with health insurance, so some employers are reportedly switching some of their full-time workers to a part-time basis. At this time, the full impact of this requirement hasn't been rigorously studied, but it certainly represents a potential shortcoming.

All in all, the jury is still out on the ACA's effectiveness. Until enough time has passed and enough data has been gathered, we won't know for sure whether the ACA is achieving its intended purposes.

they would insure the healthiest individuals and turn away the unhealthy (or they would refuse to provide insurance for preexisting conditions).

- People who have health insurance tend to overconsume healthcare, as we've seen, and their overconsumption drives up costs.

What About a Government-Run, Single-Payer System?

What we're referring to here is national healthcare, or free healthcare provided by the government to all citizens (sometimes called "universal healthcare"). Our neighbor to the north, Canada, has such a system and according to several polls, the majority of Canadians prefer their system over a US-style system. A national healthcare system would address one of the main problems we have with our current system: access. In a national healthcare system, all citizens have access to healthcare regardless of income, age, or health status.

Costs can also be more tightly controlled in a single-payer system—the government has virtually all the negotiating power, and a single payer can realize certain economies of scale that are not available in a multipayer system.

Another advantage of a national healthcare system is that health insurance can be uncoupled from employment. Most people in the United States have health insurance through their employers, but how many workers have remained in jobs they hated because they

There is much debate as to whether healthcare should be a good traded in the free market, or a primary responsibility of the government, as it is in Canada's single-payer system.

couldn't afford health insurance on the open market? From this angle, a national healthcare system in the United States would allow workers greater job mobility and could spur the formation of more small businesses.

Yet a number of problems would likely appear in connection with a national healthcare system.

- The government would have to set standards for care, and some argue that ultimately the quantity and the quality of healthcare would decline.

- People could find themselves waiting in long lines for treatment.

- Rationing could become a reality, especially as the population ages and the demand for healthcare rises.

- A national healthcare system could lead to more inefficiency and bureaucracy. The government is already famous for red tape, and it's hard to imagine that a national healthcare system wouldn't add to that.

Despite opposition and accusations of "socialism," President Obama signed the Affordable Care Act on March 23, 2010, thereby creating a federally regulated insurance "exchange."

1935

The Second New Deal

In a package designed to provide security for citizens, Congress introduces Social Security, a 40-hour work-week and the right for workers to unionize, and several other government programs designed to maintain the welfare of the country.

1945

Truman and Healthcare

Congress is called on to create a national healthcare plan, but ultimately fails to produce a bill for President Truman to sign.

1961

JFK's New Frontier

In his inaugural address, newly-elected President Kennedy uses the phrase "New Frontier." This is later used to label his administration's domestic policy that includes increased welfare assistance and emergency relief for farmers.

1944

Workplace Health Insurance

Due to a high demand for workers during World War II, US businesses begin to offer health benefits to their employees. Eventually, this leads to the employer-based healthcare system still in place today.

1956

Disabled Support

President Truman signs into law a new Social Security benefit in the form of monthly financial support for the permanently and totally disabled.

1965

Medicare and Medicaid

President Johnson picks up where his predecessors left off, calling on Congress to create Medicare. Later in the year, a bill introducing Medicare and Medicaid passes both houses, expanding coverage to senior and low-income Americans.

2010

Affordable Care Act

Legislation passes under the Obama administration designed to expand healthcare coverage to American citizens, as well as to broaden existing programs such as Medicare.

1964

Economic Opportunity Act

Legislation passes under the Johnson administration designed to reduce poverty through a series of programs ranging from vocational job training to grants for higher education in states such as California.

1996

Welfare Reform Act

Legislation is enacted under the Clinton administration designed to strengthen the effectiveness of the welfare program by stipulating limited terms on cash assistance as well as a greater emphasis on finding employment for recipients.

2015

Social Security Changes

"Vision 2025" is announced as a series of changes to the Social Security program in an effort to embrace technological advancements while also maintaining the service provided to retirees.

9 THE FUTURE OF ECONOMICS

No one has a crystal ball (though economists are sometimes criticized for behaving as if they do), and no one knows for sure how the field of economics will change over time. What is likely is that the profession will become more robust and grow more relevant to everyday life. After all, concepts and theories developed by some of the field's earliest thinkers are still relevant today. Even though certain theories have been discarded over time, replaced by better theories, or disproved by hard facts, it's likely that the field's core assumptions and theories will remain intact and continue to comprise a solid foundation for insights that future economists will uncover through their experiments and analyses. This chapter makes a few educated guesses about the future of economics, and about where economic research and thought may be taking us.

AN EVOLVING SCIENCE

Economics, like other social sciences, is a field that is always changing. Economists have been applying more and more computing power to their models, and even within the past few decades the methods and results of economic analysis have improved dramatically. All the same, economics, by its nature an evolving social science, will continue to change and develop.

Many economists today believe that economics in the future will be more empirical and quantitative than ever. As computing resources become more and more powerful, and as data sets become larger and more comprehensive, economists will be able to do many more kinds of analyses.

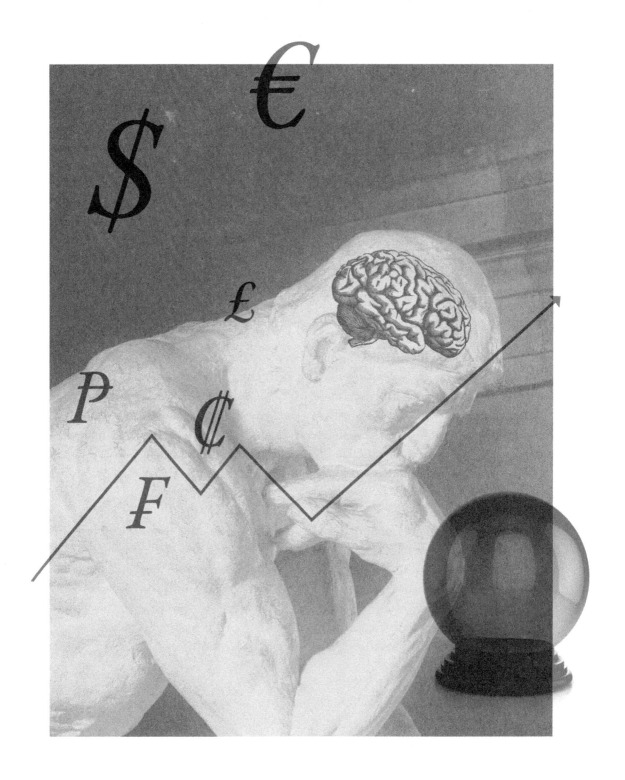

Some economists are already working with agent-based economic models, which are programmed to simulate the likely behavior of many individual actors (agents) in a market, such as producers and consumers. As behavioral economics continues to shed light on the psychology underlying different types of economic decisions, economic models are likely to become stronger and more realistic. Advances in neuroscience will probably play a role here as well. Neuroscientists are learning more about the brain all the time, and perhaps we're coming closer to the day when machines will literally be able to read minds. (Wouldn't that be a gold mine for economists who want to explore the subtleties of human decision making?)

(Opposite) Like all social sciences, economics is ever-evolving, and lessons learned from recent booms and busts will undoubtedly influence future thinking.

DID SOMEONE REPEAL THE LAWS OF ECONOMICS?

Most economists failed to see the 2007–2008 financial crisis coming, and since then the economics profession has been taking it on the chin, with critics and pundits pointing the finger at economists, and economists heaping blame on one another. For example, Paul Krugman, a Nobel laureate, accused his colleagues of "mistaking beauty for truth" and promoting a "romanticized and sanitized vision of the economy" that rendered them blind to clear dangers and left them unable to read the signals coming from the markets. In fact, whole books have been written about the failure of the economics profession (e.g., Graeme Maxton's *The End of Progress: How Modern Economics Has Failed Us* and David Orrell's *Economyths: Ten Ways Economics Gets It Wrong*). A new institute, the Institute for New Economic Thinking, was even formed in the wake of the financial crisis. Their mission involves supporting the efforts of scholars all over the world as they "change the way economics is studied, considered and taught."

In the aftermath of the crisis, many economists examining the facts may have decided that it was bound to occur, but nothing occurred in the period before the financial meltdown that violated the laws of economics. On the basis of those laws, a dozen other outcomes might have been possible as various actors in the economy responded to events. In other words, it wasn't the profession of economics that was to blame. Specific individuals, groups, and institutions were responsible for creating the environment in which a financial crisis could develop, and they took the actions that led to the crisis.

Given the severity of the crisis, however, it's easy to understand the tendency to blame economists and the field of economics, especially with heavyweights like Paul Krugman piling on. Perhaps future economic models, armed with new insights about human behavior, will be able to predict events like the financial crisis of 2007–2008.

VIRTUAL ECONOMIES AS A RESEARCH LAB

Since the first decade of the 21st century, economists have been studying certain aspects of online games like Second Life and EverQuest. These virtual worlds allow users to assume fictional identities called *avatars*. The avatars may be very different from the real-life people behind them.

In a virtual world, avatars can interact, buy and sell merchandise, form relationships, and engage in many other activities expressing the range of human behavior. Some virtual worlds even allow users to create virtual businesses, and it's fair to say that a virtual economy is one aspect of some of these virtual words.

Virtual economies are of great interest because of what they can reveal about the real economy. In some respects, a virtual economy is an excellent environment for economic experiments. For one thing, a research question that would be infeasible or even unethical to examine in real life—*What is likely to happen if interest rates suddenly double? What are the likely effects of imposing across-the-board price controls on all goods?*—can be pursued in a virtual economy without human consequences. Consider what happened a few years ago, when some Second Life users began creating banks in the virtual environment. The virtual banks, which dealt in the Second Life currency known as the Linden dollar, were completely unregulated, and in time problems began to develop in the virtual banking sector. At least one bank announced that it would be unable to meet its outstanding financial obligations. The ensuing bank run was the virtual answer to the question of what is likely to occur if a banking system is created from the ground up and left completely unregulated.

Not all economists agree on the potential of virtual economies as a research platform. Some naysayers argue that because the group of people participating in virtual worlds tends to be made up mainly of young males, it doesn't accurately represent the diverse range of participants in the real economy. It's also true that participants in a virtual world, through their anonymous avatars, tend to take more risks than they would in the real world—time served in a virtual prison is nothing like a stretch at Leavenworth.

Other economists remain hopeful about the research potential of virtual economies. They see a trend of more participation in virtual worlds, with the sample of participants becoming increasingly diverse and thus more representative of human actors in the real economy. If that trend continues, they say, virtual economies may even become the best available laboratories for economic research.

Another development that is already occurring in economics is the movement toward multidisciplinary research. At one time, research economists worked alone or perhaps with one or two colleagues who were also economists, but now it's much more common to see economists working with researchers in psychology, sociology, law, ecology, and other fields. Research of this nature is yielding and will continue to yield insights that economists would probably never reach working on their own.

One of the core ideas on which the study of economics rests is the notion of scarcity. What if scarcity was eliminated? Would the field of economics also disappear? It's an interesting philosophical question. If scarcity were eliminated, it would mean that some new technology made it possible to satisfy every human need and want, or that human beings no longer perceived the existence of scarcity. The invention of that kind of technology seems unlikely. Ceasing to perceive scarcity would require a wholesale reprogramming of human attitudes, a shift that also seems unlikely, at least in our lifetimes. If such a shift ever did occur, economics would still be relevant. There would still be reasons to examine decision making. Trade-offs would still exist because there would still be opportunity costs (e.g., should I sit here and meditate, or should I enjoy a walking meditation through the hibiscus garden?). For better or worse, scarcity is a reality that will be with us for a long time to come. Economics will also persevere as an aid to societies seeking to improve their use of resources while humankind forges ahead in a world of increasing complexity and uncertainty.

ECONOMICS

GLOBALIZATION

BUSINESS

MARKETS

BOOMS & BUBBLES

REGULATIONS

MACROECONOMICS

MONOPOLIES

HEALTHCARE

CAPITAL

GLOSSARY

absolute advantage The trade advantage a nation (or region or individual) has when it produces a particular good at a lower absolute cost.

anchoring effect A cognitive bias that describes the tendency to base a judgment on the first piece of information seen as a reference point, even if it provides incomplete or irrelevant information.

asymmetric information A situation in which one party to an economic transaction has more information about the transaction than another party. For example, if you offer your used car for sale, you have more information about the quality of the car than a potential buyer does.

behavioral economics A subfield of economics that uses psychology to examine cognitive biases and lapses from traditional rational behavior.

boom A period of substantial economic growth.

business cycles The rise and fall of business activity that occurs in an economy over time.

capital goods Goods that are produced to facilitate the production of other goods.

cartel A group of firms engaged in price fixing or other collusive behavior.

ceteris paribus Latin phrase meaning "all other things being equal."

cognitive biases Patterns or tendencies that lead people to deviate from rational decision making.

collusion The collaboration among firms in an industry to fix the price or otherwise reduce the level of competition in the industry.

common market Participating countries in a trade bloc that allow for free movement of resources between countries.

comparative advantage The advantage a country (or region or person) has when that country can produce a good at a lower opportunity cost than its trading partner.

confirmation bias People's tendency to look for or favor information that confirms what they already believe to be true.

consumer price index (CPI) An index representing a weighted average of prices that households pay for consumer goods.

contractionary monetary policy The deliberate contraction of the money supply—and increase in the interest rate—on the part of the nation's central bank.

cost-benefit analysis A type of analysis that involves comparing the potential benefits of a project or endeavor with the estimated costs.

customs union A type of trade bloc in which participating countries eliminate internal trade barriers and arrange a common external trade policy and tariff.

cyclical unemployment Unemployment that occurs due to the economy being in recession.

deflation A decrease in the overall price level over a period of time.

diminishing marginal benefit The tendency for consumers to experience less benefit from each additional unit of an item consumed.

discount rate The interest rate banks pay on loans from the Federal Reserve.

durable goods Goods that typically last longer than three years (e.g., cars, furniture).

economic union An integration of the economies of one or more nations (e.g., the European Union).

economies of scale Efficiencies or cost savings a company experiences from producing a large level of output.

efficient market hypothesis The notion that stock prices fully reflect all available information, therefore making it impossible for anyone to "beat the market."

embargo A ban on trade with a particular country, typically imposed for political reasons.

endowment effect People's tendency have to place more value on things they own compared to things they don't own.

equilibrium The intersection of market demand and market supply.

exchange rate The value or "price" of a country's currency in relation to another country's currency.

expansion The part of the business cycle that follows recession (also known as "recovery").

expansionary monetary policy The deliberate expansion of the money supply—and lowering of the interest rate—by the nation's central bank.

externalities Costs or benefits that accrue to parties outside a particular market interaction; also known as "spillovers."

federal funds rate The interest rate that prevails in the federal funds market, which is a market for overnight loans between banks.

fiscal policy A government's attempts to manage the economy through taxing and spending measures.

forecasting model A mathematical or computer model designed to predict future economic variables.

foreign exchange market The market in which foreign currencies are traded.

framing effects The way the presentation of information impacts people's perceptions of that information (e.g., the same fact may be viewed as a gain or as a loss depending on how it's presented).

free riders Individuals who want to enjoy the benefits of a public good without paying for it.

free trade agreement An agreement among two or more nations to reduce trade barriers.

free trade area An area comprising a group of nations that have entered into a free trade agreement.

frictional unemployment Unemployment that occurs due to people leaving jobs to search for other jobs, or due to students waiting to take jobs after graduation.

full employment The level of unemployment that exists when there is no cyclical unemployment (i.e., no unemployment due to recession).

gambler's fallacy The false belief that if something occurred with low frequency in the past then it is more likely to occur in the future, and vice versa.

government failure When government involvement in a market makes the outcome worse, or leads to negative outcomes in other markets.

hedonic adaptation The tendency people have to return to their usual level of happiness after major life events, both positive and negative.

hyperinflation Severe inflation.

import quotas Restrictions on the quantity of imports.

incentive A cost or benefit that motivates an individual to perform an action or make a decision.

infant industry An industry that has not yet grown to a sufficient size to be competitive with larger foreign competitors.

inflation A sustained increase in the price level over some period of time.

invisible hand A metaphor created by Adam Smith to describe the workings of market forces to coordinate economic activity.

law of demand The economic principle that states that, all else being equal, when the price of a good rises, the quantity demanded of that good falls, and when the price of a good falls, the quantity demanded of that good rises.

law of supply The economic principle that states that, all else being equal, when the price of a good rises, the quantity supplied of that good rises, and when the price of a good falls, the quantity supplied of that good falls.

macroeconomics The broad area of economics focusing on the whole economy or on the economy's large sectors.

marginal analysis A type of analysis economists engage in that involves comparing marginal benefits and marginal costs.

marginal benefit The additional benefit an economic activity or decision would bring.

marginal cost The additional cost incurred when undertaking some economic activity or decision.

market An interaction of buyers and sellers, or the medium that allows such interaction to occur.

market failure A situation in which the market produces the wrong amount of some good or service, at least with respect to society's best interests.

market outcome The prevailing price and quantity transacted in a given market.

market price The price determined by the intersection of demand and supply.

microeconomics The broad area of economics that deals with individual decision-making units, such as consumers and firms.

monetary policy The strategy and decisions of a nation's central bank concerning the nation's money supply and interest rates.

multinational corporation A corporation that has facilities in more than one country.

natural monopoly A situation that occurs when it's most efficient for one firm to supply an entire market (e.g., electric utilities).

natural rate of unemployment The lowest unemployment rate possible at a given point in time.

negative externalities Costs of a market transaction that are borne by third parties outside of the market transaction.

nominal GDP GDP that is not adjusted for inflation (or deflation).

nonuse value The economic value of an asset that is not directly related to the asset's use. For example, a forest has direct value to individuals who use the forest for timber or for recreation, and nonuse value to individuals who simply benefit from knowing the forest is protected.

opportunity cost The best alternative—or the value of the best alternative—that a decision maker did not choose in a given decision-making context.

output The amount of a good bought or sold in a market.

peak The highest point in a business cycle; at the peak, GDP and employment are at temporary maximums.

per capita GDP Output, or GDP, per person.

perfect competition A market structure in which there are so many independently acting sellers that no single seller can influence the market. Products are homogenous in a perfectly competitive market (e.g., commodities) and barriers to entry are low or nonexistent.

positive externalities Benefits of a market transaction that accrue to third parties who are outside the market transaction.

predatory pricing Charging a low price (below cost) with the intent of harming rival firms.

price ceiling A maximum legal price (e.g., rent controls).

price floor A minimum price required by law (e.g., the minimum wage is the lowest price workers are allowed to charge for an hour of their labor).

price index An index, or type of average, used to measure the overall level of prices in the economy.

prime lending rate The interest rate banks charge their most creditworthy customers.

Producer Price Index (PPI) An index that represents an average of wholesale prices.

public good A good that benefits everyone and can be used by many people without reducing its availability to others (e.g., national defense).

pure monopoly A market in which there is only a single seller.

real GDP Output, or GDP, that is adjusted for inflation (or deflation).

resource monopoly A situation in which a firm attains a monopoly by dominating all access to a necessary input.

scarcity A basic economic problem of having insufficient resources to satisfy limitless human wants.

seasonal unemployment Unemployment that occurs when seasonal workers (e.g., tourism workers) are laid off.

shock An unexpected event that impacts the economy (e.g., a natural disaster).

socially optimal outcome A market outcome that is best for society in that all costs and benefits are accounted for in the market; there are no externalities, or spillovers.

status quo bias The tendency of humans to favor the current state of things.

structural unemployment Unemployment that occurs due to structural changes in the economy, such as changes in technology or laws.

sunk cost A cost that has already been borne and can never be recovered.

tariff A tax on imports.

trade barrier Any policy that restricts free trade between nations.

trough The lowest point in a business cycle. At the trough, GDP and employment are at temporary minimums.

unemployment rate The percentage of individuals in the labor force who are not working but are actively seeking work.

BIOGRAPHIES

KENNETH ARROW

1921–

Kenneth Arrow's major contribution to economics is his work on general equilibrium theory. Arrow points out that when given enough time, a group of competitors will level the playing field, similar to how basketball team members balance each other out with their respective abilities.

Kenneth Arrow was born in New York City in 1921. He graduated from City College of New York with a bachelor's degree in science in 1940. In 1972, along with John Hicks, Arrow won the Nobel Memorial Prize in Economics for his contributions to general equilibrium analysis and welfare economics.

Today, he is the Joan Kenney Professor of Economics and Professor of Operations Research, Emeritus at Stanford University. He has also served on the Economics faculties of the University of Chicago, Harvard, and Stanford.

FRÉDÉRIC BASTIAT

1801–1850

Frédéric Bastiat, born in Mugron, France, in 1801, was not a traditional economist, but rather a journalist and commentator who devoted much of his work to criticizing protectionism, or government intervention in economic life.

While living in England during the Industrial Revolution, he wrote *Economic Sophisms*, which contains the "Candlemaker's Petition," one of his more famous witticisms. In the narrative, candle-makers in France protest against the unfair competition they face from the sun, claiming it is a "foreign competitor" and petitioning the government to block it. Clearly, he liked the idea of free markets.

Orphaned at age nine, he took up trades in commerce, farming, and insurance until he inherited his grandfather's estate in 1825, which allowed him to devote his time to writing.

As an elected member of several French political bodies, Bastiat was especially inspired by Richard Cobden and the Anti-Corn Law League in Britain and vowed to become the "French Cobden" in France.

During his lifetime, Bastiat's writings were considerably revered, translated, and republished throughout the United States and Europe.

GARY S. BECKER

1930–2014

Becker was born in Potsville, Pennsylvania. At about four or five years old, he and his family moved to Brooklyn, New York, where Becker attended elementary and high school. He later went to Princeton University, where he "accidentally" took a course in economics.

After earning his bachelor's degree from Princeton in 1951, Becker pursued graduate work at the University of Chicago, where he met and studied under the renowned economist Milton Friedman. In 1955, Becker earned his PhD at the University of Chicago with a thesis titled "The Economics of Racial Discrimination."

Gary Becker studied discrimination in economics, pointing out that discrimination hurts a producer more than it helps them, since the act of discriminating limits their market share. In 1992, Becker won the Nobel Prize in Economics for his microeconomic analysis of human behavior and interaction. In addition, Becker received the John Bates Clark Medal in 1967 and the Presidential Medal of Freedom in 2007.

RONALD COASE

1910–2013

Ronald Coase studied the way that "transaction costs"—the expenses or budget of a firm—are an important factor in developing a firm's productivity. Without them, a company would be unable to efficiently plan its economic output, since transaction costs provide the information needed to recreate conditions in the market for more profit.

Ronald Coase was born in Willesden, Middlesex, England in 1910. He earned his Bachelor of Commerce degree from the London School of Economics in 1932. In 1951, he earned a Doctor of Science degree in economics from the University of London.

Coase would go on to teach at various universities, including the London School of Economics; the University of Buffalo, New York; the University of Virginia, Charlottesville; and the University of Chicago, respectively.

In 1991, he received the Nobel Prize "for his discovery and clarification of the significance of transaction costs and property rights for the institutional structure and functioning of the economy."

IRVING FISHER

1867–1947

Irving Fisher was born in the state of New York in 1857. He attended Yale College, and graduated with a bachelor's degree in 1888. Fisher continued his graduate work at Yale, earning the first PhD in Economics ever granted by the university in 1891.

In 1930, Fisher published *The Theory of Interest,* which describes interest as "an index of a community's preference for a dollar of present [income] over a dollar of future income." Fisher's work goes on to argue that interest rates result from accounting for people's preference for immediate income, combined with the investment that will yield greater profits for them later.

In addition to his work in economics, Fisher was also a savvy businessman, earning himself a fortune in 1910 through the sales of a card-index file system he had devised. In 1926, Fisher became one of the founders of Remington Rand, Inc. and served as a board member of the manufacturing company until his death in 1947.

MILTON FRIEDMAN

1912–2006

Milton Friedman was one of the world's most influential economists. He taught at the University of Chicago's Department of Economics for over 30 years, during which time he oversaw the education of other economists and Nobel Prize winners such as Gary Becker, Robert Fogel, Ronald Coase, and Robert Lucas, Jr.

Friedman was born in Brooklyn, New York, in 1912. He earned his PhD at Columbia University in 1946. Later that year, he accepted a position as a professor at the University of Chicago's Department of Economics.

In 1957, Friedman published *A Theory of Consumption Function,* where he challenged the Keynesian perspective that government intervention can positively impact an economy.

In 1976, Friedman won the Nobel Prize for his work on monetary policy and consumption. For the remainder of his life, he researched and advocated free market capitalism. His ideas would have a significant influence on President Nixon, Prime Minister Margaret Thatcher, and President Ronald Reagan.

FRIEDRICH HAYEK

1899–1992

Friedrich Hayek was born in Vienna in 1899. Although born to wealthy parents, Hayek's privilege didn't keep him from serving in World War I, where he was a part of the artillery field.

After the war, Hayek enrolled at the University of Vienna. He earned his first degree in law there in 1921, and a second degree in political economy in 1923. During this time, he also met Ludwig von Mises, who would mentor him on the merits of classical liberalism (later called Austrian economics).

Much of Hayek's work in the 1920s and 1930s was in the Austrian theory of business cycles, capital theory, and monetary theory. In 1927, he was the director of the newly formed Austrian Institute for Business Cycle Research. He joined the faculty of the London School of Economics in the 1930s, and stayed for 18 years. Between the years 1940 and 1943, he wrote the book *The Road to Serfdom* that warned against the danger posed to freedom of state control over the means of production.

Following his time in London, Hayek taught at the University of Chicago, where he would remain until 1962. In 1974, he was awarded the Nobel Prize in Economics, along with Gunnar Myrdal.

WILLIAM STANLEY JEVONS

1835–1882

As a lifelong student of chemicals and their use, it's no surprise that Jevons was one of the early leading proponents of the "use value" theory in economics, which holds that the value of an item is determined by its usefulness.

William Jevons was born in Liverpool, England, in 1835. He first enrolled at University College in London in 1851 to study chemistry and botany, but left his studies there to work as an assayer in Melbourne, Australia in 1854. He returned to University College in 1859, to earn his bachelors and masters there.

In 1865, Jevons published *The Coal Question*, in which he analyzed the importance of coal to Great Britain's economy. A bit ahead of his time, he famously speculated that coal would eventually become a scarce resource, and that Britain's reliance on coal would prove costly.

DANIEL KAHNEMAN

1934–

Daniel Kahneman is one half of the team behind prospect theory. Prospect theory is the observation that people make more decisions by considering their potential wins rather than by considering their potential losses. Given two equal choices, people would go with the choice described in terms of what would be gained.

Kahneman was born in Tel Aviv in 1934, but at the time he and his family were regular domiciles of France. When the Germans swept into France in 1941, Kahneman and his family were forced to obey the German impositions on Jews in France. This had a profound effect on Kahneman's view of people and their complexity.

In 1954, Kahneman got his first degree in psychology from the Hebrew University in Jerusalem. He then served as a psychological evaluator in the Israeli Defense Force, where he developed methods to screen candidates for training.

Kahneman left the army in 1956 to pursue a PhD at the University of California, Berkeley, which he earned in 1961.

In 2002, Daniel Kahneman and Vernon Smith were awarded the Nobel Prize in Economics. Kahneman received his prize "for having integrated insights from psychological research into economic science, especially concerning human judgment and decision-making under uncertainty."

JOHN MAYNARD KEYNES

1883–1946

John Maynard Keynes is one of the most influential economists in modern history. After the global financial crash of 2008, many of his ideas were used to support government intervention across many of the world's major economies, including the United States, through bailouts.

Born in Cambridge, England, in 1883, Keynes attended King's College, Cambridge, where he earned a degree in mathematics in 1905.

During World War I, he was as an adviser on economic affairs for the British government. His mastery of this assignment landed him a position with the government's Treasury department. Keynes resigned from the Treasury in 1918 because he thought the Treaty of Versailles demanded too much reparation from Germany.

After resigning, Keynes returned to Cambridge. It was during this time that he published his book *The Economic Consequences of the Peace*, which objected to the Allied Powers' imposition of punitive reparations payments on Germany. His book further argued that the overwhelming debt would produce more calamities. When World War II broke out, Keynes' speculation proved right.

PAUL KRUGMAN

1953–

Paul Krugman's research is credited with bringing together previously separate branches of economic theories on world trade and consumer appreciation for diverse goods and services.

Born in Albany, New York in 1953, Krugman received his bachelor's degree from Yale University in 1974 and his PhD from MIT in 1977. Krugman has taught at Yale, Stanford, and MIT, where he became the Ford International Professor of Economics.

In 2008, Krugman was awarded the Nobel Memorial Prize in Economic Sciences for his contributions to New Trade Theory and New Economic Geography.

In addition to his research, Krugman is probably best known for his long career with the *New York Times* as an op-ed columnist, where he writes for "non-economists."

THOMAS ROBERT MALTHUS

1766–1834

Thomas Robert Malthus was a British demographer and political economist, and is often regarded as the founder of modern demography. Malthus is known for pointing out how without checks or balances, large economies would be doomed by population growth that would eventually outrun food supply and lead to famine.

As a result of these findings, Malthus promoted sexual abstinence and late marriages as ways to control or "check" population growth. However, his research was conducted before the Industrial Revolution and Malthus was unable to grasp the advances in technology that his successors would.

Nevertheless, his theory of demand-supply mismatches, which he called "gluts," paved the way for later theories about the Great Depression, as well as for the works of John Maynard Keynes.

Malthus's notion of humanity's "struggle for existence" also influenced Charles Darwin and evolutionary theory, as well as the idea of a national census.

ALFRED MARSHALL

1842–1924

Alfred Marshall was a gifted mathematician who used his mathematical skills to make the study of economics more of a science.

Marshall was born in Clapham, England, in 1842. He was raised by his parents to be a clergyman, but instead decided to pursue math and economics. Perhaps wanting to remain true to his roots, however, Marshall emphasized the importance of keeping economics intelligible for laymen.

Marshall is remembered for analyzing microeconomics, or what might be called "the everyday business of life." In particular, he looked at the relations between output, price, and supply and demand. For example, Marshall noted that when a consumer purchases more and more of an item, the item becomes less valuable. This would lead economists to observe the "price elasticity of demand," or a tool of measurement for a buyers' sensitivity to prices.

KARL MARX

1818–1883

Karl Marx is perhaps the most infamous economist in history. In the 20th century, his writings inspired such leaders as Mao Tse-tung, Vladimir Lenin, Fidel Castro, and more.

As Marx saw things, the world under capitalism was divided between the bourgeoisie and the proletariat, or the haves and the have-nots. Eventually, he said, the bourgeoisie would concentrate more wealth into their hands, leaving the proletariat with no choice but to start a revolution.

Marx was born in Trier, Prussia, in 1818. He earned his doctorate at 23 years old, along with a reputation for being a radical, argumentative figure. In 1843, Marx left Prussia after being censored by the state for his political commentary. He moved to Paris, which was an epicenter of intellectual and artistic activity at the time, but would remain there only until 1845, when the French government exiled him.

In 1849, Marx moved to London, where he would remain for the rest of his life.

CARL MENGER

1840–1921

Carl Menger was born in 1840 in Galicia, or what is now southern Poland. He is widely regarded as the father of Austrian economics, with his book *Principles of Economics* serving as the basis for this distinction.

Carl Menger recognized a system of value and use at work in economic theory, where goods, such as water, are valuable because they're useful for various purposes like drinking, showering, and watering plants. Menger observed that any labor that could produce water derived its value from the ability of the water to satisfy various wants. Today this principle is recognized as a theory of "derived demand."

Menger went on to note that people valued goods differently, or that one person's trash is another's treasure. This, he claimed, meant that in a free or capitalist market, both sides make gains. The theory would go on to influence many more economists, a group who would collectively represent the Austrian school of economics.

JOHN STUART MILL

1806–1873

John Stuart Mill was born in London in 1806. He was the son of James Mill, who himself was an economist during his day. At 16 years old, Mill found a job with the East India Company, where he would work for 38 years. His most famous essay "On Liberty" is still cited as an important reference in political discourse today.

John Stuart Mill is one of the most renowned thinkers on liberty and individual rights. Mill maintained that "the sole end for which mankind are warranted, individually or collectively, in interfering with the liberty of action of any of their number, is self-protection." In addition to his political thinking, Mill also published theories on economies of scale, opportunity cost, and comparative advantages of trade.

His book *Principles of Political Economy* was published in 1848 and was used by many economists throughout the latter half of the 19th century.

Despite his ardent beliefs in individual rights and liberties, Mill also advocated several forms of government intervention in the economy, including taxation, trade protectionism, and the regulation of working hours.

LUDWIG VON MISES

1881–1973

Along with Carl Menger, Ludwig von Mises was one of the original members of the Austrian school of economics. Mises advocated laissez-faire capitalism, or a completely free market. He staunchly opposed theories of socialism, or any other forms of government intervention in the economy.

Mises was born in Lviv, Ukraine in 1881. In 1900, he attended the University of Vienna, where he studied under Carl Menger. In 1906, Mises earned a doctorate in law from the University of Vienna and quickly began teaching afterward at his alma mater.

In 1912, Mises published *The Theory of Money and Credit*, in which he asserted that business cycles are created by the unregulated expansion of bank credit.

During World War I, Mises was a front officer in the Austro-Hungarian artillery and an economic adviser to the War Department. In 1940, fearing the Nazi influence over his homeland, he and his wife left Europe for New York, where Mises served as a visiting professor at New York University from 1945 to 1969.

JOHN FORBES NASH, JR.

1928–2015

John Nash was born in Bluefield, West Virginia. He enjoyed science experiments as a toddler, as well as looking through encyclopedias provided by his parents.

In his last year of high school, Nash entered the George Westinghouse National Competition, where he was awarded a full scholarship. He used the scholarship to enroll in the Carnegie Institute of Technology in Pittsburgh.

At Carnegie, Nash originally intended to become an electrical engineer like his father. Instead, he discovered a love for mathematics. By the time he graduated in 1948, he completed so much coursework in mathematics that the university awarded him with both a bachelor's degree and a master's degree on the subject.

Nash would go on to pursue a PhD in mathematics at Princeton. His dissertation on game theory would eventually lead economists to "Nash's Equilibrium," a concept where even after considering the moves of their opponent, no one player has any incentive to change or deviate from their strategy, hence "equilibrium."

Although Nash would eventually be diagnosed with schizophrenia, he would overcome the challenges posed by the disease in the latter part of his life. In 1994, Nash was awarded the Nobel Prize for his contribution to game theory and economics.

DAVID RICARDO

1772–1823

A Classical economist, David Ricardo was born in England in 1772.

Ricardo arrived at a number of important economic theories, including the theory of comparative advantage, which observes the way that different nations have particular advantages over one another.

Ricardo pointed out that nations *should* exploit these comparative advantages so that, for example, a nation specializing in making bread could trade with a nation that specializes in making wine, and vice versa, to develop a relation where both nations can enjoy the fruits of each other's labor.

A true master capitalist himself, by the end of his life Ricardo built a wealth of approximately $100 million dollars by today's standards. He built this fortune selling government securities as a stockbroker and loan broker.

Unlike many of the studied and well-read economists that would follow him, Ricardo didn't write his first economics article until he was 37 years old. He spent the last decade of his life as an economist.

JOAN ROBINSON

1903–1983

Joan Robinson was the first economist to define macroeconomics as "the theory of output as a whole." She is also cited as one of the Cambridge Circus, a group of economists who discussed and advanced John Maynard Keynes's *General Theory of Employment, Interest and Money*.

Robinson published her own study of the free market in 1933, with *The Economics of Imperfect Competition,* in which she showed that most industries are neither perfectly competitive nor perfectly monopolizing entities.

Born in Camberley, Surrey, England in 1903, she earned her bachelor's degree at the University of Cambridge in 1925. In 1931, she began teaching at Cambridge, where she would remain a lecturer until 1971.

For her work in the field, many economists expected her to win the Nobel Prize in 1975; however, as Robinson aged, her views moved closer to the left with books such as *An Essay on Marxian Economics* and *Marx, Marshall, and Keynes*. Although this shouldn't have kept her from winning the prize, it probably did.

MURRAY ROTHBARD

1926–1995

Unlike many economists of his day, Murray Rothbard was one of the more zealous free-market advocates of the 20th century. He wasn't opposed just to government services, but to the government as a whole, once calling it "the organization of robbery systematized and writ large."

Rothbard was born to Jewish parents in the Bronx, New York, in 1926, but grew up in west Manhattan. In 1945, he earned his bachelor's degree in mathematics from Columbia University. He would also earn his PhD from Columbia in 1956.

In the 1950s, Rothbard met the famous Austrian economist Ludwig von Mises while the latter was teaching at the New York University Business School. Rothbard would go on to write an undergraduate textbook that explained Mises's views on the free market in *Human Action*, which the Austrian would highly praise.

Although Rothbard is today considered a key advocate of the free market, he was largely shunned by most economists of his day for his often polemic and scathing criticisms of the mainstream economic theories.

JEAN-BAPTISTE SAY

1767–1832

Jean-Baptiste Say was a French economist and scholar who advanced the ideas of Adam Smith in his native France.

Today, Say is mostly credited for "Say's Law," or the notion that the value of a product is what determines its demand. For example, a bad pair of shoes could only sell for so long because eventually people will stop purchasing them. In the same sense, a pair of good shoes could sell for a long time because of the value they contain, which creates their demand.

To emphasize his point with the famous French zeal, Say asked, "How could it be possible that there should now be bought and sold in France five or six times as many commodities as in the miserable reign of Charles VI?"

Say was born in Lyons, France, in 1767. He was the first to teach a public course on political economy in the country.

E. F. SCHUMACHER

1911–1977

Before Steve Jobs and Apple minimized everything, E. F. Schumacher was the one to observe that "small is beautiful." Schumacher advanced this idea in contrast to the notion that "bigger is better."

Schumacher also advocated for human-scale, decentralized, and appropriate or small technologies that made people's lives better. His ideas made headway in an increasingly industrialized world. During World War II, Schumacher served as an adviser to the British government on employment. Following this, Schumacher became an adviser for Britain's coal industry.

Ultimately, Schumacher championed a balanced or regulated growth of markets, pointing out that excessive growth could irreparably damage the environment and deplete resources.

Schumacher was born in Bonn, Germany, in 1911. A Rhodes Scholar, he studied at Oxford University and Columbia University.

JOSEPH SCHUMPETER

1883–1950

Schumpeter might be said to have foreseen entrepreneurs such as Mark Zuckerberg of Facebook, Jeff Bezos of Amazon, and other leaders in the entrepreneurial field of the 21st century.

In particular, Schumpeter studied the way that capitalism developed what he called "creative destruction," or the process by which new and innovative products replace old ones. He also pointed out that the same process of "out with the old and in with the new" creates new markets, and with it, new forms of organization, much like the Internet developed email, which eventually led to social media.

Joseph Schumpeter was born in Třešť, Czech Republic, in 1883. In 1906, he earned his PhD in economics from the University of Vienna. In 1911, he took a professorship at the University of Graz, where he taught until the beginning of World War I.

In 1932, due to the rise of Hitler, Schumpeter left Europe and immigrated to the United States. He quickly became an American citizen and taught at Harvard until his retirement in 1949.

AMARTYA SEN

1933–

Hailing from a family of teachers, Amartya Sen was born in Dhaka, India, in 1933. He attended St. Gregory's School, where "the emphasis was on fostering curiosity rather than competitive excellence."

From an early age, Sen believed firmly in economic freedom and individual choice, finding that left-wing activism assumed too much about the needs and desires of a society made up of various individuals.

In 1953, Sen left Dhaka to pursue his doctorate at Cambridge University in England. Sen advanced quickly, so much in fact that in 1954, on a trip to India for research on his thesis, Sen was appointed Professor and Head of the Economics University at Jadavpur University. He wasn't even 23 years old yet.

In 1970, Sen published *Collective Choice and Social Welfare*, which discusses social choice theory.

ADAM SMITH

1723–1790

Adam Smith is one of the most revered economists in history. For centuries, his theory of a free market as the "invisible hand" has been a lasting image of capitalism.

Smith viewed self-interest as valuable for a society. He argued that when people pursue their own goals, they help others achieve their goals. For example, if Smith ordered a cappuccino at a Starbucks, he would point out that each of the baristas behind the counter would likely have their own incentive for making his drink. One barista might dream of owning her own coffee shop one day, while another barista might be interested in saving up for a trip to Europe. Either way, Smith would point out, before any of them could achieve their goals, they would both have to work together by helping Mr. Smith with his goal: the cappuccino.

Smith was born in Kirkcaldy, England in 1723. He published his world-famous *The Wealth of Nations* in 1776, the same year that the United States declared independence.

THOMAS SOWELL

1930—

Thomas Sowell was born in Gastoria, North Carolina in 1930, but was raised in Harlem, New York. He failed to finish high school, but after serving in the United States Marine Corps during the Korean War, Sowell pursued academics with a vengeance.

In 1958, Sowell graduated magna cum laude with his bachelor's degree in economics from Harvard University. In 1959, he earned his master's degree from Columbia University.

Since the 1970s, Sowell has taught at various colleges and universities, including Cornell, Amherst, Brandeis University, and the University of California, Los Angeles.

Today, Sowell is Stanford University's Rose and Milton Friedman Senior Fellow on Public Policy at the Hoover Institution. Though he prefers not to be labeled, he is widely considered a conservative thinker.

JOSEPH STIGLITZ

1943—

Joseph Stiglitz was born in Gary, Indiana, in 1943, and is a former chief economist at the World Bank, as well as a former adviser of President Bill Clinton's Counsel of Economic Advisers. He is most widely known for his work on asymmetric data, or the way in which two sides of information mismatch.

Essentially, Stiglitz showed how markets can make poor assumptions about the individuals they serve. In an essay co-authored with fellow economist Michael Rothschild, Stiglitz argues that people who buy insurance know more about their circumstances for insurance than the companies do, and therefore companies should offer premiums based on the information they cannot account for.

Today, Stiglitz is a professor of economics at Columbia University in New York, New York.

THORSTEIN VEBLEN

1857–1929

Thorstein Veblen was born in Cato, Wisconsin in 1857. Although he studied economics under the famed neoclassical liberal economist John Bates Clark, Veblen ultimately rejected Clark's ideas on the free market.

Veblen graduated from Carleton University in 1880. He then studied philosophy at Johns Hopkins University, but after failing to get a scholarship to support his studies there, he moved on to Yale University, where he earned his PhD in 1884.

Unlike many of his peers, Veblen's writings took a largely sarcastic tone against capitalism. He believed that the questions posed and answered by the economists of his time were too narrow.

Veblen sought to introduce more sociological perspectives into economic theory. In 1899, Veblen published his first book, entitled *The Theory of the Leisure Class*, in which he studied "conspicuous consumption," or the way in which people in capitalist societies seek to "keep up with the Joneses."

VISUAL REFERENCES

p. 11 Thomas Carlyle, courtesy of the Library of Congress, www.loc.gov/pictures/item/2004682535/

p. 13 Warren Buffet with President Obama, courtesy of the White House, www.flickr.com/photos/whitehouse/4793199789

p. 15 Wheat field & tractor (& cover, p. 100), courtesy of the Library of Congress, www.loc.gov/pictures/, www.loc.gov/pictures/item/2011631695/; computer, © Denis Rozhnovsky/Shutterstock

p. 18 Adam Smith, courtesy of the Library of Congress, www.loc.gov/pictures/item/91706325/

p. 19 Karl Marx (& cover, p. 26), © Everett Historical/Shutterstock, Communist Manifesto, © IgorGolovniov/Shutterstock

p. 22 Money production, © Sashkin/Shutterstock

p. 30 Man smoking, courtesy of the Library of Congress, www.loc.gov/pictures/item/fsa1997003411/PP/, alcohol, © Ken Felepchuk/Shutterstock

p. 32 Wall Street, © ThinAir/Shutterstock, bank vault, archive.org/stream/mnbninetyoddyearoonewb/mnbninetyoddyearoonewb#page/22/mode/1up

p. 35 Construction work, © Anne Kitzman/Shutterstock; accident © Dmitry Kalinovsky/Shutterstock

p. 36 Chili dog © Brent Hofacker/Shutterstock

p. 41 Poker chips © Ms. Abidika/Shutterstock, quarters © ET1972/Shutterstock

p. 43 House, courtesy of the Library of Congress, www.loc.gov/pictures/item/csas200802783/; for-sale sign © Andy Dean Photography/Shutterstock

p. 48 Marketplace, courtesy of the Library of Congress, www.loc.gov/pictures/item/2015650268/

p. 53 Toxic water © Belovodchenko Anton/Shutterstock; contamination symbol, © Pe3k/shutterstock; fish skeleton, archive.org/stream/naturalhistoryof1833smit/naturalhistoryof1833smit#page/33/mode/1up

p. 56 FTC building, courtesy of the Library of Congress, www.loc.gov/pictures/item/2004672464/; FTC symbol (& p. 80), commons.wikimedia.org/wiki/File:US-FederalTradeCommission-Seal.svg

p. 58 Marijuana perscription, © Brian Goodman/shutterstock; marijuana leaf (& cover, p. 67) © underworld/shutterstock

p. 60–61 Tenements, © Everett Historical/Shutterstock

p. 63 Gas station & corn field, courtesy of the Library of Congress, www.loc.gov/pictures/item/2011635869/, www.loc.gov/pictures/item/fsa2000001261/PP/

p. 66 Insignia plate for the Bureau of Prohibition, courtesy of the Library of Congress, www.loc.gov/pictures/item/hec2013006027/

p. 67 Friedrich Hayek, courtesy of the Library of Congress, www.loc.gov/pictures/item/2002719472/

p. 71 Hairdresser, © wavebreakmedia/Shutterstock; stethoscope, archive.org/stream/cu31924000231450/cu31924000231450#page/n32/mode/1up; gavel, archive.org/stream/americanbeejourn501910hami/#page/6/mode/1up

p. 73 Utility lines, courtesy of the Library of Congress, www.loc.gov/pictures/item/2013631157/; utility meters, archive.org/stream/motionpictureeleoohall/motionpictureeleoohall#page/83/mode/1up

p. 74 Gas lines, courtesy of the Library of Congress, www.loc.gov/pictures/item/2003677600/

p. 77 Standard Oil cartoon, courtesy of the Library of Congress, www.loc.gov/pictures/item/2001695241/

p. 80 Cigarettes © Andrei Shumskiy/Shutterstock

p. 81 FCC logo, commons.wikimedia.org/wiki/File:FCC_New_Logo.svg

p. 84–85 Ship & container © E.G.Pors/shutterstock; sweater, archive.org/stream/spaldingofficia02sull/spaldingofficia02sull#page/n224/mode/1up; sheep, archive.org/stream/agricultureforc000fish/#page/244/mode/1up

p. 86 David Ricardo (& p. 26), courtesy of the Library of Congress, www.loc.gov/pictures/item/90708977/

p. 88 Renminbi/Chinese banknote, © agolndr/Shutterstock; Chinese coins/yuan © Coprid/shutterstock

p. 91 European Union flag (& p. 101) © issumbosi/Shutterstock

p. 94 Factory workers, courtesy of the Library of Congress, www.loc.gov/pictures/item/npc2008007803/

p. 97 Pollution/smokestack, courtesy of the Library of Congress, www.loc.gov/pictures/item/fsa1994000008/PP/

p. 99 Immigrants, courtesy of the Library of Congress, www.loc.gov/pictures/item/fsa2000001731/PP/; statue of liberty, courtesy of the Library of Congress, www.loc.gov/pictures/item/2008679689/

p. 101 Cuban flag, © Daniel Korzeniewski/shutterstock

p. 104 Barrel of oil, courtesy of the Library of Congress, www.loc.gov/pictures/item/2003654383/

p. 106 Car production © Rainer Plendl/Shutterstock; pie, archive.org/stream/stnicholasserial351dodg/stnicholasserial351dodg#page/n383/mode/1up

p. 108–109 Flood, courtesy of the Library of Congress, www.loc.gov/pictures/item/fsa1998023548/PP/; Bastiat (& p. 124) archive.org/stream/worldsbestlitera03warn/worldsbestlitera03warn#page/1607/mode/1up; hurricane icon © doodle/Shutterstock

p. 111 Charles H. Dow (& p. 124) © Everett Historical/shutterstock

p. 113 Unemployment/meal line, courtesy of the Library of Congress, www.loc.gov/pictures/item/oem2002007808/PP/

p. 115 German woman burning money, © courtesy of the Library of Congress, www.loc.gov/pictures/item/oem2002007805/PP/; flame, archive.org/stream/campfiregirlsinmoofrey/campfiregirlsinmoofrey#page/n6/mode/1up

p. 119 Janet L. Yellen, Alan Greenspan (& p. 143), Ben S. Bernanke, Paul A. Volcker, courtesy of the federal reserve, www.flickr.com/photos/federalreserve/13896600480/in/photolist-io7D3w-naZHb1-nqrAYm-naZAsk-nvMqhY-naZzSv-naZHXE-nswwx3-nswwxU-nKeGzp-naZGFd

p. 123 Federal reserve bank © Allen.G/shutterstock; federal reserve symbol (& p. 124) © Ilyashenko Oleksiy/shutterstock

p. 125 FDR, courtesy of the Library of Congress, www.loc.gov/pictures/item/96523441/; Zimbabwe flag © Steve Allen/Shutterstock

p. 128 John Maynard Keynes © CSU Archives/Everett Collection; bubbles (& p. 138), archive.org/stream/cu31924031296126/cu31924031296126#page/n81/mode/1up

p. 130-131 Oil fields & computer (& p. 81), courtesy of the Library of Congress, www.loc.gov/pictures/item/2007661607/; www.loc.gov/pictures/item/2011636019//

p. 134-135 Squatter shacks/hooverville © Everett Historical/Shutterstock

p. 138 New housing development © David H.Seymour/Shutterstock

p. 142 Roosevelt, courtesy of the Library of Congress, www.loc.gov/pictures/item/96522736/

p. 143 Internet browser bar © dani3315/Shutterstock

p. 146 Roosevelt signing the Social Security Act, courtesy of the Library of Congress, www.loc.gov/pictures/item/00649636/, https://commons.wikimedia.org/wiki/File:Signing_Of_The_Social_Security_Act.jpg; Social Security card, courtesy of the National Archives, catalog.archives.gov/id/595679?q=social%20security; bomb, archive.org/stream/risefallofanarch00mcle/risefallofanarch00mcle#page/n168/mode/1up

p. 149 Piggy bank (& cover) © 7505811966/Shutterstock; Social Security logo, commons.wikimedia.org/wiki/File: US-SocialSecurityAdmin-Seal.svg

p. 155 Welfare office, courtesy of the Library of Congress, www.loc.gov/pictures/item/2011646496/

p. 160 Doctor's office, courtesy of the Library of Congress, hdl.loc.gov/loc.afc/afcwip.mcb0313; price tag (& cover) © MichaelJayBerlin/Shutterstock; prescription/pills (& cover, p. 66) © Hurst Photo/Shutterstock

p. 163 Canada flag © thiti/Shutterstock

p. 164–165 (& p. 167) President Obama signing the Affordable Care Act, courtesy of the White House, www.flickr.com/photos/whitehouse/4460769992

p. 166 JFK & Hoover, courtesy of the Library of Congress, www.loc.gov/pictures/item/2014648295/; www.loc.gov/pictures/item/2014648293/

p. 167 LBJ, courtesy of the Library of Congress, www.loc.gov/pictures/item/2015647172/

p. 170 Le penseur, courtesy of the Library of Congress, www.loc.gov/pictures/item/det1994023107/PP/; brain, archive.org/stream/brainasorganofmi00bast/brainasorganofmi00bast#page/381/mode/1up; crystal ball © koya979/Shutterstock

SOURCES

CHAPTER 4

Alden, William. "Goldman and Bain Settle Suit on Collusion." *New York Times*. June 11, 2014. dealbook.nytimes.com/2014/06/11/goldman-and-bain-to-pay-121-million-in-collusion-case/?_r=0.

Brinkley, Joel. "U.S. vs. Microsoft: The Overview; U.S. Judge Says Microsoft Violated Antitrust Laws with Predatory Behavior." *New York Times*. April 4, 2000. www.nytimes.com/2000/04/04/business/us-vs-microsoft-overview-us-judge-says-microsoft-violated-antitrust-laws-with.html.

Business News Daily. "10 Jobs You Didn't Know Need Licenses." May 9, 2012. www.businessnewsdaily.com/2492-occupations-requiring-licenses.html.

Federal Trade Commission. *FTC Factsheet: Antitrust Laws: A Brief History*. Accessed October 26, 2015. www.consumer.ftc.gov/sites/default/files/games/off-site/youarehere/pages/pdf/FTC-Competition_Antitrust-Laws.pdf.

Fink, Jim. "AT&T Merger with T-Mobile Blocked: Will Justice Department Compromise?" *Investing Daily*. September 13, 2011. www.investingdaily.com/11360/att-merger-with-t-mobile-blocked-will-justice-department-compromise.

Kearney, Melissa S., Brad Hershbein, and David Boddy. "Nearly 30 Percent of Workers in the U.S. Need a License to Perform Their Job: It Is Time to Examine Occupational Licensing Practices." Brookings. January 27, 2015. www.brookings.edu/blogs/up-front/posts/2015/01/26-time-to-examine-occupational-licensing-practices-kearney-hershbein-boddy.

United States Department of Justice. "Antitrust Laws and You." Last updated July 15, 2015. www.justice.gov/atr/antitrust-laws-and-you.

CHAPTER 5

Behravesh, Nariman. *Spin-Free Economics: A No-Nonsense, Nonpartisan Guide to Today's Global Economic Debates*. New York: McGraw-Hill Education, 2009.

Harrison, David. "The Economics of Immigration." *CQ Weekly*. November 24, 2012. public.cq.com/docs/weeklyreport/weeklyreport-000004178908.html.

Martini, Catherine. "E-Waste and You: A Daily Choice." *Prospect: Journal of International Affairs at UCSD*. September 10, 2012. prospectjournal.org/2012/09/10/e-waste-and-you-a-daily-choice.

Matthews, Dylan. "Five Things Economists Know About Immigration." *Washington Post*. January 29, 2013. www.washingtonpost.com/news/wonkblog/wp/2013/01/29/five-things-economists-know-about-immigration.

McCartin, Paul, Michael Bersten, and Ashley King. "Sharing Your Information: Tightening the Screws on Cross Border Arrangements." Lexology. April 1, 2015. lexology.com/library/detail.aspx?g=63f95d4f-38e1-49aa-be4f-553e3c000247.

Moretti, Enrico. *The New Geography of Jobs*. Boston: Houghton Mifflin Harcourt, 2012.

Peri, Giovanni. "The Effect of Immigrants on U.S. Employment and Productivity." FRBSF Economic Letter. August 30, 2010. www.frbsf.org/economic-research/publications/economic-letter/2010/august/effect-immigrants-us-employment-productivity.

Zavodny, Madeline. *Immigration and American Jobs*. Washington, DC: American Enterprise Institute and Partnership for a New American Economy, 2011.

CHAPTER 7

Dai, Zhonglan, Douglas A. Shackelford, and Harold H. Zhang. "Capital Gains Taxes and Stock Return Volatility." Social Science Research Network. August 11, 2010. papers.ssrn.com/sol3/papers .cfm?abstract_id=972349.

Federal Reserve Board. "The Challenge of Central Banking in a Democratic Society: Remarks of Chairman Alan Greenspan at the Annual Dinner and Francis Boyer Lecture of the American Enterprise Institute for Public Policy Research, Washington, DC." December 5, 1996. www.federalreserve.gov /boarddocs/speeches/1996/19961205.htm.

Federal Reserve Board. "Money, Gold, and the Great Depression: Remarks by Governor Ben S. Bernanke at the H. Parker Willis Lecture in Economic Policy, Washington and Lee University, Lexington, Virginia." March 2, 2004. www.federalreserve.gov /boarddocs/speeches/1996/19961205.htm.

Fuhrer, Jeffrey C., and Scott Schuh. *Beyond Shocks: What Causes Business Cycles? An Overview.* Boston: Federal Reserve Bank of Boston, November–December 1998. www.bostonfed.org/economic/conf/conf42 /con42_01.pdf.

Iwata, Edward. "Some Companies (Like Wal-Mart) Thrive Despite Recession." *USA Today.* December 5, 2008. usatoday30.usatoday.com/money/economy/2008-12 -03-recession-proof-companies_N.htm.

National Bureau of Economic Research. "US Business Cycle Expansions and Contractions." September 20, 2010. www.nber.org/cycles/US_Business_Cycle _Expansions_and_Contractions_20120423.pdf.

Smiley, Gene. "US Economy in the 1920s." *EH.Net Encyclopedia.* June 29, 2004. eh.net/encyclopedia /the-u-s-economy-in-the-1920s.

Wheelock, David C. *The Great Depression: An Overview.* St. Louis: Federal Reserve Bank of St. Louis. Accessed October 26, 2015. www.stlouisfed.org/~/media /Files/PDFs/Great-Depression/the-great-depression -wheelock-overview.pdf.

CHAPTER 8

Brandon, Emily. "5 Ways to Fix Social Security." *U.S. News & World Report.* February 13, 2013. money.usnews.com/money/blogs/planning-to -retire/2013/02/13/5-ways-to-fix-social-security.

Center on Budget and Policy Priorities. "Policy Basics: Where Do Our Federal Tax Dollars Go?" Updated March 11, 2015. www.cbpp.org/research /policy-basics-where-do-our-federal-tax-dollars -go?fa=view&id=1258.

Cingano, F. *Trends in Income Inequality and Its Impact on Economic Growth.* OECD Social, Employment, and Migration Working Papers, no. 163. OECD iLibrary. December 9, 2014. www.dx.doi .org/10.1787/5jxrjncwxv6j-en.

Dabla-Norris, Era, Kalpana Kochhar, Nujin Suphaphiphat, Frantisek Ricka, and Evridiki Tsounta. *Causes and Consequences of Income Inequality: A Global Perspective.* Washington, DC: International Monetary Fund, 2015. www.imf.org/external/pubs /ft/sdn/2015/sdn1513.pdf.

DeNavas-Walt, Carmen, and Bernadette D. Proctor. *Income and Poverty in the United States: 2014.* Washington, DC: United States Census Bureau, September 2015. www.census.gov/content/dam/Census/library /publications/2015/demo/p60-252.pdf.

DeSilver, Drew. "The Many Ways to Measure Economic Inequality." Pew Research Center. September 22, 2015. www.pewresearch.org/fact-tank/2015/09/22 /the-many-ways-to-measure-economic-inequality.

Jencks, Christopher. *Rethinking Social Policy: Race, Poverty, and the Underclass.* Cambridge, MA: Harvard University Press, 1997.

Luhby, Tami. "The Real Deal on Obamacare." CNN Money. August 5, 2015. www.money.cnn .com/2015/08/05/news/economy/obamacare-facts.

Miller, Roger LeRoy, and Daniel K. Benjamin. *The Economics of Macro Issues.* 5th ed. New York: Addison-Wesley, 2012.

Murray, Charles. *Losing Ground: American Social Policy, 1950–1980.* New York: Basic Books, 2015.

Organisation for Economic Co-operation and Development. *Focus on Health Spending: OECD Health Statistics 2015.* Paris: Organisation for Economic Co-operation and Development, 2015. www.oecd.org/health/health-systems/Focus-Health-Spending-2015.pdf.

Peter G. Peterson Foundation Staff. "Trustees Warn: Social Security Faces Major Imbalances." July 23, 2015. www.pgpf.org/issues/2015-summary-social-security-trustees-report.

Sun, Lena H., and Niraj Chockshi. "Almost Half of Obamacare Exchanges Face Financial Struggles in the Future." *Washington Post.* May 1, 2015. www.washingtonpost.com/national/health-science/almost-half-of-obamacare-exchanges-are-struggling-over-their-future/2015/05/01/f32eeea2-ea03-11e4-aae1-d642717d8afa_story.html.

Tanner, Michael D., and Charles Hughes. *The Work versus Welfare Trade-Off: 2013.* Cato Institute. August 19, 2013. www.object.cato.org/sites/cato.org/files/pubs/pdf/the_work_versus_welfare_trade-off_2013_wp.pdf.

Tanner, Michael D., Stephen Moore, and David Harman. *The Work versus Welfare Trade-Off: An Analysis of the Total Level of Welfare Benefits by State.* Cato Institute. September 19, 1995. www.cato.org/publications/policy-analysis/work-versus-welfare-trade-analysis-total-level-welfare-benefits-state.

United States Census Bureau. "Household Shares of Aggregate Income by Fifths of the Income Distribution: 1967–1998." www.census.gov/hhes/www/income/data/inequality/tablea2.html.

United States Department of the Treasury. *Income Mobility in the U.S. from 1996 to 2005.* Washington, DC: United States Department of the Treasury, 2007. www.treasury.gov/resource-center/tax-policy/Documents/incomemobilitystudy03-08revise.pdf.

United States Department of the Treasury. *Social Security Reform: The Nature of the Problem.* Washington, DC: United States Department of the Treasury, 2007. www.treasury.gov/resource-center/economic-policy/ss-medicare/Documents/post.pdf.

Walker, Elisa A., Virginia P. Reno, and Thomas N. Bethell. *Americans Make Hard Choices on Social Security: A Survey with Trade-Off Analysis.* National Academy of Social Insurance. October 14, 2014. www.nasi.org/sites/default/files/research/Americans_Make_Hard_Choices_on_Social_Security.pdf

CHAPTER 9

Institute for New Economic Thinking. ineteconomics.org.

Krugman, Paul. "How Did Economists Get It So Wrong?" *New York Times.* September 2, 2009. www.nytimes.com/2009/09/06/magazine/06Economic-t.html?_r=0.

Maxton, Graeme P. *The End of Progress: How Modern Economics Has Failed Us.* Singapore: John Wiley & Sons Asia, 2011.

Orrell, David. *Economyths: Ten Ways Economics Gets It Wrong.* Mississauga, Ontario: John Wiley & Sons Canada, 2010.

INDEX

CPSIA information can be obtained
at www.ICGtesting.com
Printed in the USA
BVOW11s0540130917
494237BV00008B/11/P